One Footstep after A.

Whatever life brings, determining to put one foot after another as we follow the Lord is the essential nature of discipleship.

I read a lot of books in the course of my work as a theological educator and sometimes I come across an idea that really sticks with, and challenges, me. One such idea, from New Testament scholar Luke Timothy Johnson, is this: 'Discipleship does not consist in a countercultural critique of society. Discipleship does not consist in working overwhelming miracles. These elements of the Jesus tradition are not made normative in the way that the pattern of obedient suffering and loving service is.'

This says to me that the visible elements of our faith, such as taking action for justice and praying for (and perhaps seeing) miracles, are of course non-negotiable in following Christ. Yet more than these things, we will be known primarily by our response to the call to obedient living, even if it costs us dearly, and to the service of others, some of whom may not share our values.

During this quarter, in which we celebrate both Easter and Pentecost, this same idea emerges in several of our sets of notes. We are called to have our hearts renewed and to live in obedience to Christ. This commitment is what changes the world. We are an army of witnesses whose lives are shaped by the hope that comes with Easter resurrection and the power given by the Spirit of Pentecost.

Mark Twain is thought by some to be the source of the aphorism: 'Life is just one ... thing after another.' In light of our call, we followers of Jesus might adapt that saying to 'life is just one faithful footstep after another.' 'Oh, let me see thy footmarks: and in them plant my own.'[1] If we can do that to our life's end, we will have been disciples. May the reading of God's Word guide our feet.

Sally Nelson
Editor

Annabel Moule
Content Assistant

John Ernest Bode, 1816-1874, 'O Jesus, I Have Promised'

ON THE COVER: Ernest Lucas gives an overview of the different kinds of wisdom literature in the Bible and how they can guide us in our daily lives.

Image credit: iStock / swissmediavision

The Writers

ELAINE STORKEY is an academic theologian and social scientist, living in Cambridgeshire, UK, who has served as theological adviser to bishops and archbishops in the Church of England. A writer, broadcaster and much-travelled public speaker, she also served as President of Tearfund from 1996 to 2013.

BRIAN RADCLIFFE is a retired English and Drama teacher, formerly minister of a Baptist church in the north of England. He also enjoys a parallel career as freelance writer (secondary school assembly scripts/drama skills as cross-curricular teaching tools).

IAN PAUL is a theologian, writer and speaker. He is Associate Minister at St Nic's, Nottingham, Honorary Assistant Professor at the University of Nottingham and a leading blogger at www.psephizo.com.

ERNEST LUCAS was a research biochemist before studying theology and has doctorates in both disciplines. Now retired, he pastored churches in Durham and Liverpool and taught Biblical Studies at Bristol Baptist College, where he was Vice-Principal. He has written commentaries on several Old Testament books.

NIGEL WRIGHT is a Baptist minister, Principal Emeritus of Spurgeon's College, London and former President of the Baptist Union of Great Britain.

ANDY ROBINSON has served as a church minister, author and evangelist. His love for preaching, alongside a call to minister, led him to Moorlands College. He has spent nearly a decade as a pastor and travels the country sharing his story and seeing God change lives.

SALLY NELSON is the Dean of Baptist Formation at St Hild College, Yorkshire, UK, where she also teaches Christian doctrine and pastoral care. She is a Baptist minister and has been the commissioning editor for *Encounter with God* since 2015.

ANNABEL MOULE is a Content Assistant at Scripture Union and the content manager for *Encounter with God*. She studied English Literature at Oxford Brookes University and Theology at the University of Oxford. She lives in Bath and is recently married to Henry.

Contents

Scripture Union is a member of the worldwide Scripture Union international community.
Website: https://scriptureunion.global

HOPE AND HOT CHOCOLATE

Joel Barwick is a youth worker with St Thomas' church in Newcastle city centre. After meeting SU Mission Enabler Geoff Brown and hearing about the Revealing Jesus mission framework, Joel became a Faith Guide. We asked him about how it's changed his outlook and experiences of mission.

How and why did you become a Faith Guide?

'Soon after I arrived in Newcastle in 2019, I linked up with SU Local Mission Partner MINE. We got some funding from SU's Good News Fund to trial some detached youth work in deprived areas. It's the one kind of youth work that's been permitted during pandemic lockdowns, so we've been able to continue doing it. And through it, I met Geoff from SU. He told me about the Revealing Jesus mission framework and invited me to become a Faith Guide – I jumped at the opportunity!

'I'm really fortunate to get great support from my church, but Scripture Union are the experts in doing mission with young people and it's so good to be able to tap into that expertise. The mission framework and the Connect, Explore, Respond and Grow phases bring some welcome structure to work with. Even as you're planning how to connect with young people, it gets you thinking down the track to how that might play out into the 'Grow' stage. It's helped me to think longer term and has given me more focus.

'You also get access to all SU's resources to use with young people at different stages of the journey. You're assigned an SU Mission Enabler (Geoff, in my case) and it's so good to have this wisdom and support. It's been great to work with other Faith Guides in the local area as well, to chat and share ideas.'

What's youth work looked like for you since you became a Faith Guide?

The pandemic's limited what we can do, so we've been doing detached youth work, going down to a park in Walker (a deprived area of Newcastle) at 6pm every Friday for an hour. There are usually between five and 30 young people, aged as young as 8. Even in torrential rain and freezing temperatures there are still young people out on the streets. We suspect they don't have the safest of places at home and feel more comfortable on the streets, even in bad weather.

It's an opportunity to be a light in their lives. We take down hot chocolate and snacks and, now they know us, they run up all excited. We might do a bit of socially distanced sport and chat, and sometimes we use SU Rooted Cards – they're great for starting conversations.

The kids are opening up to us now, and some of their situations are heart-breaking. One Friday night it was really tipping down and Spencer, this little lad of 10, turns up on his scooter, having travelled from his home about 2 miles away. We gave him a packet of crisps, but he wouldn't eat them. When I asked him why not, he said, "Because I want to give them to my mum, because we've run out of food." His mum's single, and she's got five kids under 14. Their rent had tripled that week and she had nothing left to buy food. We took them food that night and arranged for a food bank to keep them supplied. Now Spencer comes to see us every Friday in the park. We've also started a homework club with him because he struggles with school. So although it's a heart-breaking situation, we just feel as though God put him in our path.

> It's an opportunity to be a light in their lives. We take down hot chocolate and snacks and, now they know us, they run up all excited.

'Another lad, Jimmy, told me, "I just want to live at home with my mum and two sisters. I used to live with my dad, but he was too noisy." When I asked what he meant, Jimmy said, "He got drunk all the time and the other week he tried to burn the house down. So the police had to take him away." Jimmy is just 8 years old. I didn't even know what drunk was when I was 8 years old. But this is the harsh reality that these young people face. And we passionately want them to be able to experience God's love.'

Do you have any sense of how the next mission framework stages – Explore, Respond and Grow – might develop?

'We're still at the Connect stage through the detached youth work, but I can see the homework club graduating towards the Explore stage. I think other needs will emerge as we get to know the kids more. Whatever comes next has to be shaped by them. So we're really open to what it might be.

'But we're already exploring doing some new missional work involving a combination of face-to-face work in schools and online ministry. I'm trying to marry the two together and learn from what we've had to do during the pandemic. Youth mission involves going to where young people hang out, and the place where there are most young people is online. They're playing video games; they're on TikTok; they're on Instagram; they're on Snapchat. Even children as young as 8 have their own phones. So there's a harvest field online and we need to be speaking the gospel there and sharing it effectively. Those young people are going to be learning about the world and life through worldly things unless we go on to those digital platforms and teach them differently.

'You still need the face-to-face work though. You can do the Connect stage with young people online, but I really feel you need a personal relationship for the Explore and Respond stages of a faith journey. And you need that too for the Grow stage – you need someone to disciple you, to walk alongside you and help you to mature as a Christian.'

Would you recommend being a Faith Guide?

'Absolutely. I think when it comes to youth work, some churches aren't sure what they can offer or where to start. It can be a really big block for them. 'Having the Revealing Jesus mission framework and someone to lead you through putting it into practice is hugely beneficial. I can pick up the phone to Geoff, sound him out on my ideas and he'll help me improve on them. Not only that: he'll come and lend a hand too. At the moment he's out every Friday night, chatting to the young people right alongside me – I'm continually blown away by how servant-hearted SU people are.'

Find out more about the Revealing Jesus mission framework and what it means to be a Faith Guide!

We're looking for volunteers, commissioned by their local church and supported by Scripture Union, to act as Faith Guides for children and young people without church backgrounds, walking alongside them as they journey to faith. Could that be you, or someone you know? Find out more and apply at su.org.uk/revealingjesus

A shorter version of this story first appeared in Connecting You, *SU's free quarterly supporter and prayer magazine. Subscribe for free to learn more of how God is moving in the hearts and lives of children and young people today:* su.org.uk/connectingyou

Using this Guide

Encounter with God is designed for thinking Christians who want to interpret and apply the Bible in a way that is relevant to the problems and issues of today's world. It is based on the NIV translation of the Bible, but can easily be used with any other version.

Each set of readings begins with an *Introduction* to the section you are about to study. The *Call to Worship* section at the start of each note should help you consciously to come into God's presence before you read the passage. The main *Explore* section aims to bring out the riches hidden in the text. The *Growing in Faith* section at the end suggests ways of applying the message to daily living.

The *Bible in a Year* readings at the foot of the page are for those who want this additional option.

JESUS, FAITHFUL TO THE END

The final five chapters of Matthew's Gospel take us to the conclusion of Christ's earthly ministry, culminating in his death and resurrection. Chapters 24 and 25 begin this section with the disciples admiring the magnificence of the Temple in Jerusalem – and Jesus prophesying its destruction. This theme of the end times describes cataclysmic events which will herald Christ's return. References to the Hebrew scriptures give warnings against false prophets and living without heed to the judgement to come. Christ's followers are urged to be ready for his impending return. Parables of the ten virgins, the returning master and the sheep and the goats drive home the need to live before God with preparedness and compassion.

The remainder of the Gospel concentrates on the last week in Jesus' life, beginning with the plot against him and continuing through to the final outcome. We watch as Jesus is anointed by an unnamed woman; we see him eat a last symbolic supper with his disciples; we hear him struggle with intense fear in isolation in Gethsemane; and we shudder as he is betrayed in the garden to those who hate him. We follow Matthew's account through Jesus' arrest, phoney trials, torture, crucifixion, death and burial, recognising the injustice and ruthlessness of his enemies, the abnegation of responsibility by the Roman ruler and the weaknesses of his friends.

Matthew's narration is powerful. As he takes us through these events and relationships he unfolds the magnitude of the contrast between the world's evil and God's love. The empty tomb and Christ's resurrection demonstrate the overwhelming power of that love over sin and death. The story ends with the risen Jesus appearing first to the women and then to the men, commissioning them to make disciples of all nations. As Jesus speaks to his disciples, we know that he speaks to us too. His concluding message is one of challenge and promise. The world needs us as witnesses to God's love, and we need Christ's constant promised presence to work through us.

Elaine Storkey

Matthew 25:14–30

In God's Service

Lord, help me to shut out all distractions now, so I may become focused on your Word and grow in wisdom.

A talent was a weight, valuable according to its metal. We don't know its value in this story, but we do know that the talents were distributed unequally in proportions of five, two and one. Jesus was not reinforcing status, hierarchy or inequality in this story, but simply describing how things are. Humans differ; each one is gifted differently from others. What matters is not the quality or number of our gifts, but what we do with them.

The fundamental problem with the useless servant was his attitude. Lacking self-confidence, he could have committed himself to learning more and trying harder; but didn't. Instead, he grumbled and complained. He was bitter about his lot, envious of those better endowed and resentful of his master. Yet the master placed no impossible demands on him. He asked him only to work within his ability and develop what he had. By putting his

talent in a hole, to be returned intact but unchanged, the servant ignored the trust placed in him. The outcome was 'use it or lose it' – loss for him and gain for the two who worked hard.

We see these attitudes in the church as well as in society. Sometimes we prefer things to stay as they are, rather than use our gifts to effect and direct changes around us. The result is that things change anyway, but we are not part of it. We can also run away from responsibility because we don't have the gifts that others exhibit. Yet those who have many gifts still have to work to develop them. The master isn't rewarding a class of elite indolent people. God has entrusted all of us with gifts and he asks everyone to use them well. We're called to think, plan, pray and act, so we can be useful citizens in God's kingdom.

What are the gifts God has given you? How might you develop your talents more for Christian service?

BIBLE IN A YEAR: Joshua 1–3; Psalm 37

Matthew 25:31–46

Oblivious to Blessing

Lord, stop me, challenge me, guide me and direct me. Please speak through your Word today, so I can serve you better.

The story of the sheep and the goats is a chilling parable at many levels. Those who come before the judgement seat of God are divided not by what they profess or believe, but by the way they put their faith into action. The judgement is not related to the correctness of their theology or the sermons they've preached, but to their compassion. Those affirmed by God are motivated by love for others, especially the vulnerable. Those rebuked are indifferent. The story thus warns against apathy and complacency and challenges the illusions we might have about ourselves.

Notice how easy it seems to be to win God's approval. He is not commending any great achievement these people have attained. The things Jesus focuses on are not costly, except in terms of time and effort. They are simple actions that anyone can take. We can all share food and drink, welcome strangers, provide clothing and visit the sick and imprisoned. These deeds require only kindness and humility. They are also unselfish. Those who reached out to others were not doing so to get something back. They didn't want applause or to become the focus. They didn't see themselves as good. Their actions were the natural, thoughtful responses of those who care about others.

The other group didn't care about others and were oblivious to their needs or suffering. They imply that if they'd known they would be doing these things for God's approval they would have done them. That's not compassion. It's still self-centredness. The parable is a challenge to us all. God sees our actions and knows our hearts. He wants us to serve him. We do that best not just by preaching to others, but by sharing our faith in action, motivated by genuine, consistent neighbourly love.

Are there things you need to do to show love to someone in need today? Pray that God may guide you to someone who needs your compassion and kindness.

Psalm 40

Deliverance Will Come

Lord, teach me the patience of the psalmist, that I also may wait on you and hear your voice.

David is very conscious here of his fragility and need. Facing problems from many directions (v 12), he has enemies who would rejoice in his downfall (vs 14,15) and he's under no illusion about his own spiritual state. He is poor and needy (v 17), his sins can easily overwhelm him (v 12). The metaphor of the 'slimy pit' (v 2) sums up powerfully the difficulty any of us can have in maintaining spiritual stability in troubled times and finding a firm place to stand.

What keeps David going is not confidence in himself, but in God. The whole psalm acknowledges God's protection over him, expressing thankfulness for God's mercy and deliverance. God lifts David out of the mud, saves him, delivers him and puts a song in his heart. Here is a clear Old Testament picture of God's grace and love. God is not fixated on sacrifices or rituals (v 6) but on faithfully showing love and mercy towards us. God is the active one. David's part is simply to open his heart to receive him. This is what empowers David. He wants to praise God and publicly share his goodness. He wants others to know God's faithfulness so that God can be glorified.

David never denies his own neediness. Even after extolling God's greatness and victory, he returns to his own fragility and his never-ending dependence on God. We can do the same. There is nothing incompatible between knowing our own weakness and failures and praising God for all we are worth! How often in your life have you felt discouraged by relationships or situations and been dragged into despondency? The reminder here is that we need never stay there. God can place our feet on firm ground. God can engulf us in his love and give our hearts new gratitude and praise.

What things get you down most? Name them before God and ask him to give you the peace and stability that lifts you above them.

BIBLE IN A YEAR: Joshua 6,7; Romans 11

Benevolence and Betrayal

Thank you for this time, Lord, when I can let go of the thoughts that clutter my mind so that I may feed on your Word with trust and joy.

Today's passage has something of a see-saw feel. We have a statement of fact from Jesus, then a sinister echo from the scribes and Pharisees. We have an act of generosity and trust from a woman, then an act of greed and treachery from a disciple. It all happens in the context of the Passover preparation. For Jesus, the Passover brings the time to be handed over to his enemies. For the scribes and Pharisees, it brings the time to arrest him, away from the crowds.

Matthew's account of a woman anointing Jesus parallels those of Mark and John. Luke's account is different. As in other Gospels, her action here causes consternation, this time over the alleged extravagant waste. The plea that the money involved could have been given to the poor cuts no ice with Jesus; he calls her action 'beautiful' (v 10). It's a symbolic, loving preparation of his body for burial.

This action from the unnamed woman is in great contrast to that of Judas who, unlike her, knows Jesus and has lived in close relationship with him. The woman gives, pouring out love. Judas takes, exchanging Jesus for 30 pieces of silver. Judas prepares Christ's body for burial too, but through infidelity and betrayal.

Today, people often ask whether Judas could really be held to blame. Since Christ's death was essential for the salvation of the world, surely Judas' betrayal was theologically necessary? It's a false dilemma. What Judas did was profoundly wrong, and he chose to do it. God brought salvation through Christ's death, but it could have happened in any number of ways. God does not put sin in people's hearts – neither Judas' nor ours. We are responsible for our sin. Judas himself bore the guilt of treachery and betrayed the one who loved him.

In many parts of our world commitment to evil has terrible consequences. Pray for those places God lays on your heart and for sustained Christian witness there.

BIBLE IN A YEAR: **Joshua 8,9; Romans 12**

Matthew 26:17–25

A Painful Passover

Thank you, Lord, that I can read your Word and hear your truth in peace and freedom. I pray today for those who cannot.

We know nothing about the man who provided the place of hospitality for Jesus and his disciples to celebrate the Passover. He may never have known the significance of their gathering. Most of the disciples didn't either, at least not fully. Judas had clearly managed to hide what he had been doing from his fellow disciples. So they ate and drank together in apparent peace. Judas, however, could not hide his intentions from Jesus and he soon knew that Christ was fully aware of them. The public announcement that one of them would betray Jesus was clearly a party-stopper.

It feels unnerving that each of the disciples asked Jesus if it could be him. Could they all be capable of betrayal? Though eleven of them had no such intention, they lacked sufficient confidence in their own righteousness to be able to rule it out. In true humility, they were able to recognise their ability to sin. Only Judas asked the question hypocritically, for he knew the answer and Jesus confirmed it. Christ's reference to one who 'has dipped his hand into the bowl with me' (v 23) indicates the closeness of their relationship and the depth of the betrayal.

Many of us are able to hide our sins and failings from others, even those who are very close to us. Which of us is a truly open book to our friends and family? Which of us has no thoughts or attitudes which we would want sometimes to conceal from others? Many people are very skilled at hiding and live with all kinds of deceit and pretence. Judas found he could not hide from Jesus and nor can we. God sees our hearts and knows our motivations. May we live at peace in that reality.

'Search me, God, and know my heart; test me and know my anxious thoughts. See if there is any offensive way in me, and lead me in the way everlasting.'[1]

[1] Ps 139:23,24

BIBLE IN A YEAR: **Joshua 10,11; Psalm 38**

Matthew 26:26-35

Christ's New Covenant

Thank you, Lord, for showing us how we should pray and celebrate your love for us. May your Holy Spirit lead me in deeper worship today.

Jesus' actions are often full of symbolic meaning. His entry into Jerusalem showed him as Servant King, to be received with welcome. This meal is similar. The Passover feast was a celebration of the Jews' deliverance from captivity. The blood of the sacrificial lamb placed on their doorposts would ensure their safety as the angel of death passed over. Now, through his words to his disciples, Jesus identified himself with the Passover lamb. It's his body, his blood that will bring safety and deliverance. In sealing the new covenant with God, Jesus discloses himself as Saviour from sin. Like his disciples, we receive Christ's body in faith, symbolically, in communion.

On the Mount of Olives, Jesus needed to warn the disciples about what lay ahead. It must have been very uncomfortable to hear his prediction that they would not stay the course. After the meal and joyful singing, Peter's confidence was strong. He would never desert Jesus! Jesus knew better, however, and his prophetic word, offering the details of Peter's denial, probably stayed with that disciple for ever.

Jesus' compassionate attitude towards the disciples is extended to us. He knew that they would desert him, but didn't reproach them. Even when Peter contradicted him, Jesus didn't respond with contempt. He simply described the outcome with clear accuracy. Jesus knows that our weaknesses will lead us to sin. Peter thought his love for Christ and his faith in him were strong enough to withstand anything. He was wrong. We can easily be self-assured about our own discipleship. Yet, like Peter, we are only safe when we replace confidence in our own strength and ability with the humility of depending only on God.

What are the areas of weakness in your life where you need more dependency on God? Pray now that God will increase your trust in him.

BIBLE IN A YEAR: **Joshua 12-15; Romans 13**

Matthew 26:36–46

Loneliness and Fear

Dear God, fill my heart with compassion and my mind with gratitude. Help me, through what I read today, to appreciate Jesus even more.

It is time for Jesus to pray. One unnamed friend had provided him with the upper room, now another gives him access to an olive garden where he retreats with Peter, James and John – men who witnessed the transfiguration. Jesus knows he is going to die a barbaric death. He must overcome his fear and place his trust in the Father. This is not easy. He wrestles in prayer, pleading three times for some other way. We see the agony and intensity of Jesus' praying. Luke's Gospel describes it like sweating great drops of blood.[1] He empties himself of any residual self-will before finally conceding 'your will be done' (v 42).

We see the loneliness of Gethsemane in this passage. The three disciples are asked to keep watch with him, but they fail miserably. When Jesus finds them sleeping he characteristically asks them now not to pray for him, but for themselves. Their lack of commitment to him in his hour of greatest need makes them more vulnerable to attacks from the evil one. The impact on Jesus is to increase his sense of isolation. He has to face the terror in the loneliness of his own soul. So, they sleep on, and Jesus disturbs them only when the time for his betrayal has come.

The disciples arise from their sleep; Jesus arises from his knees. They go on to an ordeal with which Jesus has wrestled, but for which the three others are completely unprepared. Jesus is ready, having been in deep prayer. This speaks to us of its great importance. Jesus has subordinated his own human will to God's higher authority and found the peace that will enable him to face death. For us to be able to stand in defiant courage before evil, we too need first to have knelt in fervent prayer before God.

Let us pray today for all those who are wrestling with evil and injustice, and ask God to draw them close to the courage of Christ.

[1] Luke 22:44

BIBLE IN A YEAR: **Joshua 16–19; Romans 14**

Matthew 26:47–56

The Kiss of Violence

Dear God, help me to experience the leading and empowering of your Holy Spirit so that your Word may come alive in my head and heart today.

The story of Jesus' betrayal is more complex than it seems. Judas has given crucial information to Jesus' enemies, especially the time and place when he would be away from crowds. Judas offers to identify him with a kiss of greeting. Yet Jesus would need little identification. He was well known. When Judas does kiss Jesus, the word in Greek changes. It's not a kiss of 'greeting' but one of 'repeated passionate embrace'. Why? Some scholars suggest that Judas wanted Jesus to make a show of divine strength, to call down angels and demonstrate his power. Whatever Judas' ultimate motives were, however, Jesus calls him 'betrayer' (v 46).

Jesus' arrest symbolises the warfare of peace and truth against violence and lies. No peace comes with Judas' kiss. Instead, he effectively heads up a lynch mob, reputedly sent by the chief priests and elders, but clearly outside the law. It becomes quickly obvious that violence is not Jesus' way; it should never be ours. In our own world, we find so often that violence brings only further violence. Jesus rebukes the disciple who attacks the servant, and restores the man's ear.[1] In front of armed men, he makes it clear that he could call angels to blast his enemies – but he doesn't. For us, too, Christ's way is that of peace, not military might.

Although it was costly, Jesus made his own response to the arrest. Nothing forced him to come to Jerusalem for Passover. He could have exposed Judas and cut out his betrayal. In the garden, he could have quietly slipped away before the mob arrived. Although his life would be taken brutally from him, he laid it down by choice. Foretold by prophets and in the plan agreed between him and the Father, Jesus' death was given for you and me. God's purposes are worked out only by sacrificial love.

What does it mean to you in your daily life and relationships to be a follower of the Prince of Peace?

---

[1] Luke 22:51

BIBLE IN A YEAR: **Joshua 20–22; Psalm 39**

Matthew 26:57–68

The Court of Injustice

Lord, thank you that you are a God of justice. Open my eyes to see those areas of our world where injustice flourishes and how Christians can bring change.

Jesus faces the mockery of a trial alone. His disciples have fled; Peter follows and watches from a distance but offers no help. The trial seems to have taken place quickly, presided over by the high priest at his house with the Sanhedrin already assembled. Sanhedrin regulations, however, decreed that criminal cases should be tried during daytime and at their own meeting place in the Temple precinct. No criminal trials should occur during Passover. This trial seemingly involved multiple violations of Jewish law.

Two witnesses, examined separately, were required to make compatible allegations. We don't know how many futile attempts were made, as the Sanhedrin scoured for evidence. Eventually, two people attested that Jesus claimed he could destroy and rebuild the Temple in three days. This was a distortion, both of his prophecy and about his own death and resurrection on the third day. Jesus chose to remain silent before the lies.

Following the next question, Jesus might have walked away a free man if he had remained silent or denied he was the Messiah. Saying 'yes', invited the charge of blasphemy and a sentence of execution. Yet his answer went even further. He quoted Daniel 7:13 and applied its account of the triumph and glorification of the Messiah to himself. Jesus knew full well what he was doing. The high priest's symbolic garment-tearing and the court's violent scorn confirmed the death penalty. The injustice Jesus faced has been echoed in the lives of his followers through the ages. A reminder of that frenzy and hatred, accompanying the rejection of Christ as God's anointed one, faces so many of his faithful witnesses in the persecuted church today.

What sort of injustice and oppression might we have to face as the price for staying faithful to Jesus? Pray now for protection and courage to stand firm.

BIBLE IN A YEAR: **Joshua 23,24; Romans 15**

A Prophetic Psalm

Help me, Lord, to bring to you, now, whatever burdens I am carrying, so that I can experience a lightening of my load.

David is weighed down with three burdens: his struggle with a guilty conscience, ill-health and betrayal by a close friend. In these battles, David experiences a sharp contrast between God's care for him and other people's malice. His enemies have written him off, expecting his death, but he is confident that God will sustain and restore him, despite his sins. He identifies himself with those who have integrity (v 12), who show concern for the weak and know God's approval (v 1). Now that he is weak himself, he is ready to experience, firsthand, God's care for the helpless.

David is doubly betrayed by others. Some people pretend to be friends but come only to learn things they can use against him (v 6). Others share in the slander and false witness. However, the greatest betrayal is from someone close to him (v 9). All these have resonances in the New Testament. Jesus is betrayed by people who twist his words, by the crowds who turn against him and by Judas who 'shared [his] bread' (see v 9). In John's Gospel, Jesus quotes this verse at the Last Supper,[1] when, having received bread, Judas leaves. Yet David's confidence in the ultimate mercy and justice of God is again justified: echoed so powerfully and finally in the Messiah's own victory over evil and death.

We too can share confidence in God, whatever burdens we are carrying. We can admit our faults to God and rely on the peace of forgiven sins. We can ask God to give us concern for the weak and make them a priority in our Christian service. Wherever we are weak, we can know God's restoring strength and his blessings on our daily lives. The victory that David glimpsed and Jesus knew is ours also, through God's eternal love.

Pray for those you know who struggle with weakness and heavy burdens today, that they will be drawn to the strength and compassion of God.

[1] John 13:18

BIBLE IN A YEAR: **Judges 1,2; Romans 16**

Matthew 26:69-75

Cowardice or Courage?

Lord, help me to know myself better through this reading today. Please show me how I can overcome the weaknesses and shortcomings that you reveal in me.

Peter's denial of Jesus comes so soon after his profession of unflinching loyalty that it's easy to believe that his commitment was shallow. His immediate denial to the maid, and his curses when his Galilean accent identifies him to everyone, lead to his disowning Jesus completely. Only after his third denial does the cock's crowing remind him of Jesus' prediction. Some suggest this may not have been an actual cockerel crowing, but the name given to the trumpet call heralding the changing of the Roman guard. Whatever the source, the sound makes Peter painfully aware that Jesus knows him better than he knows himself.

William Barclay has a charitable view of Peter, seeing him less a coward than a man of 'heroic courage'. He didn't flee with the other disciples but, in his desperate desire to stay close to Jesus, put himself at considerable risk. He followed him into danger, into the very courtyard of the high priest's house, and though he denied knowing Jesus to protect himself, his love for Jesus compelled him to stay there. His love was evident in tears of bitter remorse when he realised how badly he had let Jesus down.

Any of us, facing perils as followers of Christ, might find Peter's emotional and spiritual struggle in our hearts. We take comfort from the fact that, despite his cowardice, Peter's faith in Christ never wavered. Scholars believe that the reason this painful story is in the Gospels is that Peter told it to the early church. He wanted everyone to know that even though he failed Jesus in the hour of greatest need, he was forgiven, restored and entrusted with leadership in the church. What Jesus did for Peter, he can do for us. Peter's story is not of human failure, but of Christ's redemptive and healing love. It applies to us all.

Romans 8:38,39 assures us that nothing in all creation can separate us from the love of God in Christ Jesus.

BIBLE IN A YEAR: **Judges 3,4; Mark 1**

Matthew 27:1–10

The Tragedy of Judas

I pray, Lord, for more wisdom to understand the effects of sin in our world and for protection from your Holy Spirit against its power in my life.

Despite the speed and success of their manipulations, the Sanhedrin could not pass the death sentence on Jesus. This had to be pronounced by the Roman governor and carried out under his authority. The Temple elders now had to construct some political charge which Pontius Pilate could not dismiss. In the Temple precinct, Judas watched the destructive plan unfold and realised, with huge remorse, the outcome that was now inevitable. The chief priests, however, were in no mood to engage with his regret – he had served their purposes. The money he no longer wanted was contaminating and could only be used to buy a burial ground for unclean bodies.

Flinging blood money into the heart of the Temple was the action of a desperate man, now confronted with the gravity of his sin. Although he could hurl the money back, he could not take his own action back. Sin cannot be undone. Its consequences can rarely be avoided. Judas finally recognised the gravity of his betrayal. He had exposed an innocent man to the injustice of those who hated him. Jesus' life would end on a brutal Roman cross. No wonder Judas could no longer live with himself. His suicide marked the realisation that his existence was now intolerable.

Judas lived long enough to hate what his sin had bought him. He did what he thought he wanted, but came to detest it. This is a common human experience. Sin creates a longing which, when fulfilled, can so easily become a loathing. Sin can captivate us, also, and take us into bondage. Most of us are able, thankfully, to reach out to God and seek forgiveness for our wrongs. Jesus prayed from the cross even for those who killed him. We, unlike Judas, can rejoice that God's grace is greater than our sin.

Lord, help us not to hold on to sin, but to have the humility to confess it before you and receive your forgiving grace.

BIBLE IN A YEAR: **Judges 5,6; Psalms 40,41**

Matthew 27:11-26

Governing Responsibly

Teach me, Lord, how your Word speaks into every period of history and area of our world. May I find its power more effective today.

Most people before a judge would have their case well worked out, ready to answer the charges against them. An innocent person, especially, would have prepared a cast-iron rebuttal. Yet, Jesus again says nothing. Even Pilate is surprised, urging him, without success, to make some response. Pilate, however, was unlikely to be familiar with Isaiah 53:7 or its significance in his court: 'he did not open his mouth; he was led like a lamb to the slaughter, and as a sheep before its shearers is silent, so he did not open his mouth.' Here, surely, was the one of whom the prophet spoke.

Pilate was impressed by the integrity conveyed in Jesus' calmness and authority. Having seen many revolutionaries, Pilate knew that Jesus was not one. He also knew he was being used by the Jewish religious elite to get rid of someone who made them uncomfortable. The festival custom of prisoner-release provided the clear answer. The crowd would make the obvious choice between this Jesus Messiah and the violent brutal criminal Jesus Barabbas. When the crowd refused Jesus' release, Pilate simply gave in. In allowing them to pronounce a sentence of death, he simply abdicated all responsibility.

Washing his hands of the matter did not absolve Pilate from the injustice of his actions. None of us can walk away from the responsibilities that are ours, for God will hold us accountable even if worldly systems don't. Injustice today thrives through dereliction of duty by those who should judge impartially. Pilate retained responsibility for Jesus' crucifixion, even though he handed it to the crowd. We, too, remain answerable, as Christian neighbours or citizens, for the level of injustice we ignore or encourage.

Let us pray for more people of integrity, truth and Christian wisdom to lead our nations today.

BIBLE IN A YEAR: **Judges 7,8; Mark 2**

Matthew 27:27–44

Crucifixion is Barbaric

Lord, as your Word takes me into the cruelty and evil of human structures, show me how I can rely upon you to empower me to stand against them.

Nothing humane exists in crucifixion. The flogging of Jesus would have left him bleeding, lashed and barely able to function. The soldiers epitomise the worst in human nature in their awful degrading humiliation and scorn. Nothing resembling respect or compassion was offered to Jesus, but instead mockery, violence, ugliness and hatred. Even forcing Simon of Cyrene to carry his cross was no concession. Jesus was so weak he could not have otherwise made it to execution. Yet carrying Christ's cross may have been a life-changing experience for Simon, for Mark names his sons, suggesting they were known as Christian followers.[1]

We are horribly familiar with the details of the crucifixion – the impaling of Jesus' body on the cross, the nails driven through his hands, his refusal of the drugged wine to deaden the pain, the stripping of his clothes and the soldiers casting lots. Since Jesus was crucified alongside two criminals, the caption signifying him as 'King of the Jews' (see v 37) spoke only of irony to passers-by.

Even now, the religious leaders could not leave him to die quietly. They joined in the mockery with the crowd and convicts. Unbelief is rampant in any age, ours included. People in our society are just as ready to ridicule faith in Christ. His powerlessness on the cross signifies defeat; cynicism proclaims the emptiness of Christian hope, as people still echo the sneering of that Good Friday crowd. Yet, unbelief always misses the point. It was Christ's persistence in staying on the cross that saw his mission through. It's his victory as Son of God that has drawn millions to him throughout the ages. It's his death that brings life to us today.

We are challenged today to witness to Christ in an age of growing unbelief. Pray now for greater wisdom in knowing how.

[1] Mark 15:21

BIBLE IN A YEAR: **Judges 9,10; Mark 3**

Matthew 27:45–56

Depths of Darkness

'Nothing in my hand I bring, / simply to your cross I cling; / naked, come to you for dress; / helpless, look to you for grace'.[1] Thank you, Jesus.

Jesus hung on the cross for about six hours, the darkness of the last three culminating in his cry of abandonment by God. This cry was penned by King David centuries earlier[2] and foreshadows many of the elements of the last few hours of Jesus' life. Not understanding, well-wishers in the crowd offer him vinegar and they wait, thinking he is calling on a prophet. After his final shout, 'It is finished',[3] he dies – and an earthquake brings cataclysmic damage to Temple and tombs, terrifying the guards. Suddenly, they're convinced that Jesus was the Son of God.

What really did Jesus mean by quoting Psalm 22? It seems such a cry of Godforsakenness. Some suggest that Christ is identifying fully with human hopelessness and suffering, but it is also a cry of cosmic spiritual truth. As Jesus was sacrificing himself and being made sin for us,[4] he was experiencing the outcome of sin in separation from the Father. His forsakenness was at a level we shall never know. Christ suffered and died to bring grace to us who don't deserve it. It's pictured symbolically, with the Temple veil torn and the Holy of Holies opened up to ordinary human access. A new relationship with God can be ours through Christ.

It is fitting that the passage ends with the story of dedicated women. A male disciple had betrayed Jesus, another denied him and most had fled, yet the women remained to the end. They speak to us of the reality of faithfulness, despite perplexity, doubt or distress. Their confusion must have been greater than most of us have ever known, yet they give us courage. We too can stay close to Jesus in the worst of circumstances of our lives and not waver in our hope.

Are there people around you who need your Christian encouragement today? Why not pray and reach out?

---

[1] AM Toplady, 1740–1778, 'Rock of Ages' [2] Ps 22:1 [3] John 19:30 [4] 2 Cor 5:21

BIBLE IN A YEAR: **Judges 11,12; Psalms 42,43**

A Sealed Tomb

Please, Lord, reveal new gems of truth in your Word today so that I might see them clearly and that they may deepen my faith.

It probably suited both the Romans and the Jewish leaders to hand Jesus' body to Joseph of Arimathea. For the Romans, it avoided leaving a decaying corpse to be eaten by animals. For the Jewish leaders, the Passover was not overshadowed by a hanging crucifixion victim. Being rich, Joseph probably had some status but, more importantly, he had a tomb. Not far from the place of execution, it seems to have been newly hewn out of the rock. Tombs were expensive, so it was generous of Joseph to provide his for Jesus. He did not know that he would soon get his tomb back!

Matthew details that the tomb was very thoroughly closed up. Joseph himself rolled the massive stone into the groove in front of the opening. Once sunk in, the stone could not be rolled back by one person alone. Then, at the request of the chief priests, Pilate made it doubly secure.

In sealing it with rope and wax at either side of the entrance, the soldiers ensured that no one could tamper with it. Posting a guard was the final security; the body, imprisoned inside, could not be removed. No one would spread false rumours of resurrection.

Every age has had its theories about the body and the tomb. Some people today suggest that Jesus wasn't really dead, but was later rescued. Yet no one there had any doubt that Jesus was dead. He had been flogged, tortured, impaled, hung for hours and speared. What his enemies feared was either disciples snatching his corpse, or that a miracle might really happen. The wonderful thing for us is that they took such care to keep the body in, ruling out all normal possibilities of exit. We are left with the knowledge that God's miraculous power is the best explanation for what happened next.

Frank Morison's classic book *Who Moved the Stone?*[1] resulted from an attempt to disprove the resurrection. It is a wonderful read for every generation.

[1] Frank Morison, *Who Moved the Stone?*, Faber and Faber, 1930

BIBLE IN A YEAR: **Judges 13,14; Mark 4**

Matthew 28:1–10

Hope Fulfilled

Lord, I pray for the Holy Spirit's presence in my reading of your Word, to feed my heart and mind with your love and grace.

For the women, the Sabbath must have felt like an endless wait. They knew they must anoint Jesus' precious body, but the question of how to get into the tomb was formidable. When they finally arrived with prepared spices, they were utterly bewildered by what confronted them. Shocked, numbed soldiers in disarray – and an angel seated on the rolled-back stone – conveyed an unexpected reality: no body to anoint. As they entered the tomb and saw for themselves that it was empty, the angel's words sank in. They were to tell the disciples that Jesus had risen and would meet them in Galilee.

When Jesus, very much alive, suddenly appeared to them, their old roles seem turned on their head. Instead of being those who fulfilled personal, domestic tasks of embalming a corpse and carrying messages, they became the first witnesses to Christ's resurrection. Yet it was surely fitting. The faithful women who had been at the cross and tomb now saw and worshipped the risen Christ. They were appointed personally by Jesus, as the first evangelists to proclaim the good news of the most world-changing event in history: that he was indeed risen from the dead.

Jesus empowered the women to be the people he was calling them to be. As his newly appointed ambassadors, they could let go of fear, rejoice in his victory and proclaim the gospel. So can we. Jesus' calling is not limited to background, age, time or culture. He can empower all those who believe and trust in him to be witnesses of his resurrection. God anoints us today to share the calling of those first eyewitnesses in proclaiming the good news of Christ's sacrificial love and resurrection power.

Let's thank God for choosing us to tell the message of Jesus' amazing resurrection. Let's pray that we may be faithful witnesses to his victory over sin and death.

BIBLE IN A YEAR: **Judges 15,16; Mark 5**

Matthew 28:11–20

The Greatest Commission

Lord, thank you that your Word is truth and that Jesus is the Way, the Truth and the Life. Help me to live today rejoicing in him.

Manipulation and injustice dominated everything the religious authorities did to Jesus. William Barclay says that they used treachery to lay hold on him, illegality to try him, slander to charge him to Pilate and bribery to silence the truth about him – but, despite all their efforts, they failed. The false story about the theft of Christ's body folded, as the Holy Spirit communicated the power of Christ's resurrection to hearts across the world. Over the past two millennia, billions of people have believed through God's Word and have based their hope on Christ's victory over sin and death. God's truth triumphs over the lies of Satan, and those in bondage to evil.

When Jesus gave his commission to followers gathered in Galilee, he told them to make disciples of all nations and teach them the way of Christ. It must have seemed an incredibly tall order to a small group of Jewish men who had spent their entire lives within a small part of the earth. Christ spoke to both those who believed and those who doubted; his commission was not based on the strength of faith of his followers, but on his own power.

Without Christ's power, the disciples could accomplish nothing. We know that ourselves, as God commissions us afresh to continue the work passed down to us. We do not rely on our strength and we are not disqualified by our doubts, because all power in heaven and earth is given to Jesus. Our weakness is made perfect in Christ's strength, even when evil seems to flourish and truth brings persecution, but we need to hold on to the promise he made to his disciples, for it is true for us today. Christ will indeed be with us always, even to the end of the world. His love will sustain us.

May God be with you and bless you as you seek to serve him in the work he has given you, or as you are being prepared for something new.

BIBLE IN A YEAR: **Judges 17,18; Mark 6**

Scripture Union

IT'S YOUR MOVE

YOUR SECONDARY SCHOOL SURVIVAL GUIDE

- Over 1 million children helped to settle into a new school through this series.
- New content and design for a new generation.
- Includes a survival guide, survival journal and survival stories to help children adapt to a new school.
- Additional content available online.

Scripture Union

IT'S YOUR MOVE

YOUR SECONDARY SCHOOL SURVIVAL GUIDE

ORDER FROM **YOUR LOCAL CHRISTIAN BOOKSHOP**
ORDER FROM **SCRIPTURE UNION: 01908 856006**
ORDER ONLINE **WWW.SCRIPTUREUNION.ORG.UK**

DO YOU WANT THE GOOD NEWS OR THE BAD NEWS?

When we refer to someone as 'a Jeremiah', we're implying that they are the bearer of bad news. So, in our exploration of these chapters, we shall often hear the word 'Woe!', we shall return constantly to the condemnation that Judah has broken the covenant with God and we shall shiver at the repeated, terrifying descriptions of the enemy at the gates, crouching to pounce in retribution.

Jeremiah's prophetic ministry speaks into a time of political and religious crisis in the southern kingdom of Judah, during the reigns of Josiah, Jehoiakim and Zedekiah. Caught between the competing powers of Assyria, Egypt and Babylon, Judah is a vassal state, attempting to balance tactical alliances with an urge for independence. Jeremiah's message makes the point that mere structural and political change is not enough. There must also be a change of heart, particularly among the influential classes: the king and his officials, the priests and the prophets who advise him. There must be an obedient return to the covenant relationship with God.

There is no coherent chronological pattern to these prophetic words. This is an anthology, a freewheeling, stylistically varied collection of utterances. Sometimes it's by no means clear who the speaker might be. The imagery is vivid: the LORD is the faithful husband and Judah the adulterous wife; Israel and Judah are like two contrasting sisters; the advance of the ruthless power of the surrounding states is threatening and imminent. Yet Jeremiah himself appears as a gentle, compassionate patriot. He is not a natural bearer of such a harsh message and he takes the national situation personally, clearly broken-hearted as his words are rejected. Maybe he's the appropriate model for us, speaking truth to power in an age when much of society and government appears increasingly deafened. Like him, we may often feel isolated and lonely, but the message is still the same: a change of heart and an obedient life are the only foundations of a stable, just society.

Brian Radcliffe

The Set-up

Lay aside your preconceptions and invite God to open these chapters to you in a new, vivid and relevant way.

Like a Hollywood blockbuster, the book of Jeremiah opens with the set-up: the context and the potential narrative. The book spans over 40 years and the reigns of three kings of Judah: Josiah, Jehoiakim and Zedekiah. Jeremiah's backstory is given: his priestly heritage and, more importantly, his role in a divine plan that existed from before his conception. Next comes the commission: to go where God sends him, to speak the words God commands and to face the fears within and without, knowing that God is with him. Our hero's initial response is that of many a biblical character chosen by God: 'Who? Me?' Finally, however, with God's encouragement, he turns to face the task ahead, symbolised in two visions: the evil hordes pouring out of the north towards the gates of Jerusalem, and God (like the branch of an almond tree) overlooking the drama.

Jeremiah's expectation in life was to become a priest. A man was a priest by birth into a priestly family. A prophet, by contrast, was a prophet by God's choice, a spokesman (or occasionally a woman) for a specific time. Jeremiah's prophetic responsibility was to deconstruct the social, political and religious life of Judah in the hope of rebuilding and replanting. The nation, despite the reforms initially introduced in Josiah's reign, had drifted into idolatry.

There is a prophetic imperative given to all Christian believers. We are to speak truth to power, not merely within the confines of our church community but also in local, national and international contexts. God overlooks, empowers and protects us as we highlight anything that devalues his perfect plan and purpose for his creation.

Choose an issue of injustice. What prevents you from speaking out? Youth? Age? Insignificance? Lack of education? Invite God to touch your mouth and to provide his words.

Young Love Gone Sour

Bring to mind the moment you came to faith. Thank God for the people, the place and the realisation involved in that experience.

My wife and I recently celebrated our golden wedding anniversary. We are happily married after 50 years. This, sadly, is not the situation pictured here. The young love and early devotion to God (v 2) of the nation of Israel have not merely waned, they have been wilfully torn to shreds. Evil is rampant, vividly symbolised as dry wells (v 13), wild, uncultivated vines (v 21) and lustful, indiscriminate adultery (vs 23,24,33). As the injured party, God asks, 'What did I do wrong? Did I not treat you right?' (see vs 5,6,8). He says that no other nation changes its gods (vs 10,11) and points to the consequences already experienced by the northern kingdom (Israel) of this breakdown (vs 14-17). In the end he focuses on the nub of the matter: 'you ... have no awe of me' (v 19). This is not just a human relationship. This is the fearful Lord, your God.

Jeremiah is commanded to proclaim this word in public to the whole city of Jerusalem. A response is required from each citizen. However, the message is directed particularly at those who have influence and decision-making power within the nation: the priests, the Levites (the law-givers), the rulers and the prophets (v 8). It's concerned with politics, bipartisan treaties with pagan neighbours (v 18), national and international issues. Again, he is implying that this is not merely a human issue. This is the Lord their God.

'The fear of the LORD is the beginning of wisdom'.[1] It's right to remember that our relationship with God, precious and comforting as it may be, is more than an emotional attachment. We are privileged to love, to follow and to obey the one who is the Creator and Sustainer of the universe.

Meditate on what God has the power and the right to do, to you and the whole of this world. Thank him for Jesus, who makes us his children.

[1] Prov 9:10

BIBLE IN A YEAR: **Judges 21; Mark 7**

Jeremiah 3

The Half-hearted Sister

Ask God to reveal to you your unfulfilled ambitions, your frustrations, your dissatisfactions and your unredeemed failures. Be totally honest with yourself.

These words from the Lord to Jeremiah are relatively easy to place in a historical context. They are given during the reign of King Josiah over Judah, a period of religious reformation in the southern kingdom. The population of Israel, the northern kingdom, is largely in Assyrian exile, driven there by Sargon II in 722 BC. Jeremiah listens as the two kingdoms are pictured as a pair of married sisters alike in their lecherous adultery. Israel had initiated the lifestyle. Judah had followed. Pretending to honour the Lord in religious reform, Judah actually plays the harlot's game.

Jeremiah is told to address the words of prophecy not directly to Judah, but overtly northwards to Israel. Nevertheless, the message is just as clearly addressed to the southern kingdom. Jeremiah paints a picture of all that God will do for Israel: he will provide trustworthy leadership and Jerusalem will be the centre of a united kingdom, incorporating both Israel, returned from exile, and Judah. There is one condition. Israel must acknowledge her guilt. The issue is idolatry, reliance on the gods of wood and stone imported from surrounding cultures. The choice is clear and simple: does your trust lie in the Lord or in foreign gods? The sinner is called to repent.

How does it feel, therefore, to stand in Judah's shoes? 'Faithless Israel is more righteous than unfaithful Judah' (v 11). To God, the pretence of worship (v 10), the disregard for the significance of sin (v 9) is almost worse than outright rejection. It's a heart-stopping realisation, as these are the same shoes we should beware of standing in ourselves. A superficial faith is no way to reach the promises God has in store for us.

Let the Spirit walk with you through the issues highlighted in the earlier prayer. Acknowledge your weakness, your misunderstanding, your guilt. Invite Jesus to forgive, to heal and to empower.

BIBLE IN A YEAR: **Ruth 1,2; Mark 8**

A Lifebelt in the Storm

Come into a time of confession, acknowledging before God your falling short of his righteous expectations of you.

My mother has told me vivid stories of people's reactions as they heard the wail of air-raid sirens echoing through the streets of World War II Liverpool. Men, women and children dropped what they were doing and fled for the shelters. Only air-raid precaution and emergency services members stayed out. God tells Jeremiah to sound the alarm. Powerful images describe the imminent attackers: a lion, a scorching wind, chariots like a tornado and horses like eagles. There is overwhelming noise, earthquakes, the promise of catastrophic destruction. All leadership collapses in the face of such violent attack. The aftermath is pictured in further sombre descriptions: the land a waste and void desert, depopulated, the cities desolated ruins. The light of the nations has been put out.

In these verses it's often hard to distinguish between God's voice and Jeremiah's own confused and emotional reactions. He questions God's apparently contradictory words to the nation (v 10), through the mouths of other prophets. He recoils from the anticipated horror, his heart races, he is torn apart with anguish (v 19). Our own hearts go out to Jeremiah and the agony of his task in sounding this warning to those among whom he lived.

I need something to clutch on to when faced with a passage like this, a lifebelt in a storm of impending judgement by a righteous God. Jesus' disciples had just such an experience.[1] Two features of this story give me reassurance. First, Jesus was in the boat, in the storm with them, as he is always with us. Second, his authority exceeds the strength of any storm and his loving sacrifice of himself covers our failings in the face of his Father's righteousness. Our hearts have been washed from wickedness (v 14).

Sit with hands open and receive the forgiveness of God into your own mixed-up life. Listen for the words he wants you to take into his mixed-up world.

[1] Mark 4:35–41

BIBLE IN A YEAR: **Ruth 3,4; Psalm 45**

Jeremiah 5

A Glimmer of Light

Darken the room in which you find yourself. Close your eyes. Experience the limitations, the oppression of the absence of light. Invite the Lord to enter.

God sets Jeremiah a task. He is to scour the streets of Jerusalem for someone, just one person, who does justice and seeks for truth. What does he find? He discovers arrogance among those who wield power (vs 3,5) and ignorance among the uneducated (v 4). There is rampant, depraved immorality (vs 7–9) and complacency that God will do nothing (v 12). Finally, there is the root cause: the serving of foreign gods in the land God has given. God's response through Jeremiah's voice is like a flame-thrower. An invader will come and lay waste the kingdom of Judah.

Yet, in this judgement, there exist two glimmers of light. First, there is the sense that God longs to pardon his disobedient people (vs 1,7). He is a God who is both righteous and loving. He can abide no disobedience, no rejection, no evil, but he longs for his people to return to him. He wants a mutual, loving relationship. That is his nature. Second, there is the indication that destruction will not be total: 'do not destroy them completely' (vs 10,18). He will not eradicate Judah.

This commentary was written during a period of deep global darkness. On the one hand, the pandemic threatens every nation. On the other, insurrection has taken place in what were deemed stable democracies. In addition, the Christian faith is under threat worldwide from ignorance, complacency and greed. Yet God has not changed. He is not asleep. He is not detached from his creation. While his righteous judgement condemns, his merciful love, demonstrated in Jesus, stretches to every corner. 'The light shines in the darkness, and the darkness has never put it out.'[1]

Hold up before God five people – local, national or international figures – who you believe are doing justice and seeking truth. Pray that they may be lights in the darkness.

---

[1] John 1:5, GNB

BIBLE IN A YEAR: **1 Samuel 1–3; Mark 9**

Psalms 42,43

Don't Give Up

Acknowledge to God the ups and downs of the past week, both in tackling a tough set of Bible passages and in life in general.

Peter Gabriel, on his album *So,* sings a magnificent duet with Kate Bush entitled 'Don't give up'. He takes the role, in the verses, of a man who has no fight left, a loser who can't take any more. She, in the refrain, sings a message of hope, reassurance and encouragement: 'Don't give up'. Similarly, these two psalms give us three stanzas in which the singer, deep in depression, laments his separation from God with vivid imagery of drought (42:1), an overwhelming flood (42:7) and public humiliation (42:3,10; 43:1). Yet each time there's the refrain 'Put your hope in God' (42:5,11; 43:5).

This could be Jeremiah's theme song. Beset on every side with the demands of God and the realities of life, he could easily be tempted to give up. These psalms give a tidy response. First, self-pity is rebuked. Why do you let yourself feel this way (42:5,11; 43:5)? Second, there is the recollection of better times, processing to the Temple and the experience of God's love, or an acknowledgement of God's nature as a stronghold, the source of light and truth. Finally, there is a clear statement of intent: 'I will praise', 'I will remember', 'I will go to the altar', 'I will sing and play praise to God'.

Spiritual depression is not uncommon. Most, if not all, of us will have experienced times when we've felt distanced from God. Prayer seemed unanswered, praise merely words, our faith was running on empty. Here we have a structure for responding to such times. First, we recognise and reject a focus totally on ourselves. Second, we remind ourselves of who God is and what he's done. Third, we commit ourselves to a course of action, moving towards him. Then, let the living water flow.

Make a clear note of the three stages of recognising, reminding and recommitting. Place the note where you will see it every day.

BIBLE IN A YEAR: **1 Samuel 4–6; Mark 10**

Jeremiah 6

The New Religion

Thank God for those who lead worship and preach within your local church.

There is nothing cheap about the religious practices in the city of Jerusalem during Jeremiah's time. There is an abundance of frankincense, sweet spices, burnt offerings and sacrifices (v 20). Religious ritual is in fashion. Yet what is the result? 'They dress the wound of my people as though it were not serious' (v 14). The effect of these rituals is superficial. Even the prophets and priests are on the make, complicit in the corruption of society (v 13). There is no depth, no sincerity, no moral change. They don't even blush (v 15)! It is ritual for show, ritual as routine.

The writer Robert Macfarlane has a book entitled *The Old Ways* in which he explores trusted traditional routes around the British Isles: those that follow the wooded valleys, the accessible mountain passes and the safe river crossings.

So God implores his people to return to the Mosaic tradition, to live by the essence of the Law (v 16). He even promises his satnav: prophetic voices that warn of the dangers ahead (v 17). Yet all God receives in response is rejection.

I take great stimulus from creative initiatives in worship and teaching. I like my worship music to mirror my Spotify choices. I find that visual images enhance written words. I enjoy drama and interviews. I value all of these, but not for their own sake. They have no value unless they draw me closer to God and challenge me. They are to refine me (vs 27–30), to highlight my imperfections, my unhelpful traits and my errors, and to turn me to repentance and to receiving God's forgiveness and peace. This is the deep healing God sent his Jesus to bring to his wounded creation and wounded people.

Take an old (and battered?) prayer book or liturgy. Relish the words from a past generation and use them to enhance your personal prayer time.

BIBLE IN A YEAR: **1 Samuel 7–9; Mark 11**

Inside/Outside Religion

Picture the entrance door to your place of worship. Imagine friends entering. Pray for God's peace and blessing on them today.

Stepping through a doorway into a different land is a recurring theme in children's (and some adult) literature. *The Lion, the Witch and the Wardrobe* by CS Lewis is a well-known example. In today's passage, Jeremiah is told to station himself at the entrance of the Temple in Jerusalem and to convey God's command that those who enter must look back over their shoulders before looking forward to their worship. Behind them, in their daily lives, they are involved in injustice, racial and social prejudice, murder, idolatry, theft, adultery and perjury. Then they intend, miraculously, to enter the Temple and rejoice in their redemption, parroting words of praise and worship to the Lord. Two wildly contrasting worlds (v 11), which God deems unacceptable.

Jesus points out the same contradiction centuries later,[1] but by his time the wickedness has entered even the Temple courtyards themselves. Dishonesty and greed have become the norm. It's not unknown today, whether we picture Mafia godfathers at the first communion of their children, the parroting of prayers for political gain or hypocrisy within the local church. For some, although thankfully not for all, what they do outside the doors of a place of worship belies what they express inside.

'Walk in obedience to all I command you' (v 23). That's the starting point that God gives us as we gather inside to worship. It has been suggested that all churches should have written, on the inside of the doorway leading out into the life of daily work and daily relationships, the word 'ENTRANCE'. What God asks of his people is to live out his principles of justice, truth, honesty and love in a broken world. Faith in action is a seven-day activity.

Pray the words of the Lord's Prayer as you would in church. Then repeat the prayer, meditating on what it means to your life outside your church community.

---

[1] Mark 11:17; Luke 19:46

BIBLE IN A YEAR: **1 Samuel 10,11; Psalms 46,47**

Jeremiah 7:30 – 8:19

Save the Children

Bring to mind six children you know, from your family, your neighbourhood, your church community. Pray for their protection and guidance this coming day.

Today we plumb the depths of darkness. The people of Judah, not content with installing foreign idols in the holy places (v 30), in a horrific perversion of the rituals instituted by the Lord, are now carrying out child sacrifice (v 31). No wonder today's passage ends with the bleak echo of three voices over the charnel house of the valley of Hinnon: a distraught Jeremiah (8:18), a confused, deserted population (v 19a) and the almost despairing cry of a rejected God (v 19b).

I find these verses agonisingly relevant today. They provoke images of starving children with wide eyes and swollen bellies, of North African pre-teenagers huddling in tents beneath Paris underpasses, of Nigerian school pupils taken at best as hostages, at worst to be trained as child soldiers and sex slaves. Are these any less horrific than the child murders of Jeremiah's time?

Jesus is very clear about the place of children in the kingdom of God. In Matthew 18:1–6 he explains that children demonstrate the essence of the kingdom itself (v 3). They are the model of simple faith (v 4) and are to be safeguarded and nurtured (v 6). Significantly, to adults he says that a child is to be received as if we are receiving Jesus himself (v 5).

Child sacrifice illustrates how far Judah has fallen from God's direction. They have devised a horrific form of worship that had not even entered God's mind (7:31). Maybe our attitudes to our children can be a useful guide to our closeness to his purposes.

Search for news stories about children. Respond to each child with the heart of Jesus. Actions as well as words are to be encouraged.

BIBLE IN A YEAR: **1 Samuel 12,13; Mark 12**

Jeremiah 8:19 – 9:26

Community in Breakdown

Recall special holidays and thank God for the refreshed feeling you experienced as you returned home.

Some years ago I contributed to a file of secondary-school assemblies entitled *Community Cohesion*. Today's passage paints a picture of a community that would benefit from such a file. As so often, sexual impropriety comes top of the list of ills (9:2), but much of the community breakdown has its roots in what people are saying to one another. They bend the truth (v 3), inform on one another to gain an advantage (v 4), slander and deceive (v 8). This has now become endemic (vs 5,6). Jeremiah has two options: to stay and endure deep, personal anguish (v 1) or to retreat to a desert refuge (v 2).

I, too, have sometimes longed to get away from the incessant daily diet fed by the media. I'm tempted by the lure of TV programmes such as Ben Fogle's *New Lives in the Wild* or *Escape to the Country*, setting up home in rural isolation, with their promise of relief from the stress and complexity of living in a community. Over past decades my wife and I have at times welcomed the option of such a bolt-hole, whether a caravan, a cottage in France or our present motorhome, but it has only ever been a break, so that we might then return, refreshed, to life where we belong.

Community cohesion does not come through political and sociological strategies, scientific and philosophical analyses, or power and wealth (v 23). It can only come through knowing God in the relationship given to us by Jesus and in understanding his ways through the gift of the Holy Spirit (v 24). Equipped in this way, it's our task to introduce our communities to his enduring love, his justice and his holy righteousness. Where we belong. We are God's glue for his cohesion.

Choose three situations that grieve you within your local community: dispute between neighbours, a local injustice, personal slander, for example. Pray about them, then listen for what God invites you to do.

BIBLE IN A YEAR: **1 Samuel 14,15; Mark 13**

Jeremiah 10

Scarecrows in a Field

Sit in silence for a moment. What comes into your mind? Tasks that need doing? Exciting opportunities? Compelling concerns? Let God enter and take pride of place.

Let's give some credit. It takes a lot of time, skill and effort to construct an idol. It involves the skill of the lumberjack and the sculptor (v 3), the goldsmith and the joiner (vs 4,9), the seamstress and the dresser. And all to what end? These idols cannot speak, cannot move; they have no power at all. They won't ever come alive like the scarecrow Worzel Gummidge in the children's story or Dorothy's companion in *The Wizard of Oz*. They have no moral conscience like Pinocchio. They can do neither good nor evil (v 5). So why has the nation given them such priority?

By contrast, look at the Lord. Verses 12 and 13 vividly paint a picture of the true God, who is powerful, wise and creative. He is not merely living, he is everlasting and his moral authority is unquestionable (v 10). So why has the nation drifted away from him? With a hint almost of exasperation, God declares that he will 'hurl out those who live in this land' (v 18). He has had enough.

In his song 'Peace will come',[1] the folksinger Tom Paxton recognises the world's need of renewal and sings 'and let it begin with me'. So too Jeremiah starts with himself. He acknowledges his wanderings and subjects himself to the judgement of God (vs 23,24). We too need to recognise our personal moral weakness as we reflect on the moral weakness of our own nation. Our idols may not be made of wood and stone, but any motive, attraction, obsession or preference that influences us above the Lordship of Jesus Christ is their equal. For the rich young man facing Jesus, it was wealth.[2] For us there are infinite other possibilities.

Play the Tom Paxton song 'Peace Will Come' (available both on Spotify and YouTube) and use it to lead into a period of meditation, repentance and forgiveness.

---

[1] Tom Paxton, 'Peace Will Come', 1972   [2] Matt 19:21,22

BIBLE IN A YEAR: **1 Samuel 16,17; Psalm 48**

Don't Shoot the Messenger

Take a prayer walk (real or imagined) around your local area. Bring to God issues, both individual and social, that come to mind.

'Let's get back to basics,' says God. 'When you left Egypt, I asked you to listen to me, to obey and therefore to become my precious people. I promised to be your God and to lead you into the perfect homeland' (see vs 4,5). 'That's all it takes.' Simple? As we have read, it wasn't simple at all. The people, tempted by the religious practices of surrounding nations, turned increasingly to the worship of idols. Thus the disobedience of the two kingdoms, Judah and Israel, results in the judgement and punishment of God (vs 7,8,11).

Jeremiah's pronouncement of this message has been utterly consistent. He never held back. As a priest, he probably also departed from local devotion to the shrines of imported idols, in line with reforms initiated earlier during the reign of King Josiah. It would be the logical course of action, the consequence of the words given from God. Jeremiah, however, in his naivety, is unprepared for the reaction his pronouncements have provoked (v 19). It is stark: either he shuts up or he will be silenced. That's the threat.

God's command to all people today is as simple. Jesus puts it succinctly: 'Love the Lord your God with all your heart and with all your soul and with all your mind and with all your strength ... Love your neighbour as yourself.'[1] That's the message we're given to convey to those where we live, with whom we work and with whom we share relationships. So how do they react to our words and actions? Do they even see God's command as relevant to them? How well do we cope with disagreement, scorn or even anger? Or are we tempted to compromise on Jesus' words or even to keep our utterances to ourselves? What calibre of messengers are we?

Return to the thoughts generated on your prayer walk. Decide on three conversations, emails or phone calls that you should make, as God's messenger.

[1] Mark 12:30,31

BIBLE IN A YEAR: **1 Samuel 18,19; Mark 14**

Psalm 44

Confused

Pray for the suffering, persecuted church throughout the world.

Many a football club has its stories of the good old days. An FA-cup giant-killing feat, or a promotion to a higher division – so why is this team now locked in a desperate fight to avoid relegation? Similarly, the psalmist asks on behalf of his beleaguered nation why, after generations of military success, are they now suffering defeat after defeat? With a note of sarcasm, he asks why God is asleep (v 23). We almost expect the heavens to open and a bolt of lightning to strike at such disrespect!

For me, the psalms are the most brutally honest part of the Bible. In addition to worship, praise and thankfulness, they express the exasperation and confusion of relating to an omnipotent God. Why does he act the way he sometimes does? Why does he apparently not act at all, particularly in relation to suffering and injustice in the world? Is it because our lifestyles and our prayers aren't up to scratch? Well, no. God would have told us if that had been the case (vs 17–22). Is it because we've been tempted to trust in 'my bow' and 'my sword' (v 6) rather than 'your right hand, your arm, and the light of your face' (v 3)? Maybe, because we've all occasionally tried to take things into our own hands, to hurry things along. However, that's not the whole answer.

The psalm gives no easy answers. It ends with a miserable, oppressed man grovelling in the dust and reaching out to the one certainty, that God's love never fails (v 26). It's a cliffhanger. Thankfully, we know what the culmination will be. Paul quotes this psalm before writing his great assurance that nothing can separate us from the love of God in Christ Jesus.[1] Thank God for that.

Remind yourself of the times God has clearly shown his love to you. Fold them around you. Feel the security they evidence. Take confidence to face the day.

[1] Rom 8:35–39

BIBLE IN A YEAR: **1 Samuel 20–22; Mark 15**

Get a Grip!

Read Psalm 13:1–4. Be honest with God about what you find frustrating and confusing about life today.

Every company has a complaints procedure. When a product doesn't live up to expectations, then we can complain, with a view to recompense. Jeremiah has a complaint: life's not fair! It doesn't add up. God himself is just and true (v 1a) yet unjust and evil people thrive (vs 1b,2). Jeremiah is doing his best (v 3a), so, by implication, why is he under so much attack? He wants his money back! He wants proper punishment to be enacted. At times, looking at the world around me, I feel the same. Why does God not intervene in corruption, injustice and crime? I am confused and frustrated, even a little angry. What is God's response?

God's words are enigmatic: 'So you think things are bad now, Jeremiah? It will get worse. And it will get personal' (see v 6). 'Jeremiah, get a grip.' God then provides some perspective, from his own point of view. He has been rejected by his own chosen people and consequently invaders have wreaked chaos in the perfect land he gave them. Yet even in the desolate ruins, they have not given him a thought (v 11). How does Jeremiah's complaint compare with that? So, I must admit, my petty frustrations, complaints and confusions pale into insignificance when placed alongside God's cosmic burden.

Thankfully, we end on a much more uplifting note, with an international dimension. Addressing the invaders, God issues a message of hope, although there are conditions attached. Just as they seduced Israel and Judah into worship of Baal, so God invites them to worship him. Compassionately, in a war-torn world he offers a stable, multinational homeland (v 16). It's a hint of the commission Jesus gave to his disciples (and therefore to us): 'go and make disciples of all nations.'[1] Let's never allow that hope to die.

Concentrate on the international dimension of your prayers of intercession. It may require research and persistence, but the effort is what God asks of us.

---

[1] Matt 28:19

BIBLE IN A YEAR: **1 Samuel 23,24; Mark 16**

Jeremiah 13

The Stinky Underpants

'May these words of my mouth and this meditation of my heart be pleasing in your sight.'[1]

There is a classic piece of advice given to budding writers: 'Don't tell me, show me.' What a character does communicates much more than what they merely say. Taken a step further, theatre and film give the opportunity for the audience to view as well as listen to the message or story. God tells Jeremiah to create two pieces of street theatre. First, the linen belt (the Israelite equivalent of underpants or knickers), an intimate garment which, if not washed but left in the air, becomes contaminated. Second, an excess of wine results in a drunken, senseless mob. The intimate relationship of the Lord with his chosen people has been spoiled by exposure to foreign influences, so they have become a senseless, violent rabble, unable to rule or be ruled. God's condemnation of Judah continues in three vivid pictures: the traveller on the twilight road (v 16), the command for the king and the queen mother to step down (v 18) and the shameful public exposure of a woman, with a hint of sexual violence (vs 22,26). God doesn't mince his words or censor his imagery.

Jesus spoke a lot of words, but he also illustrated what he said by his actions. Crowds were fed, sick people healed, tables turned over; finally, a stone was rolled away and he, a dead man, appeared alive again. The early church acted out Christ's teaching as they ate, prayed, healed, shared and created a resurrection community.[2] Actions spoke louder than words, as is seen in the resulting numbers of those who came to join them.

It's not always easy to speak Jesus' words into other people's lives. Sometimes it's easier, and more effective, to be like Jesus to them. Actions speak.

Follow the words of the hymn 'Take My Life'[3] and ask God to turn good intentions about time, physical abilities, finance, intellect and love into significant public actions.

---

[1] Ps 19:14 [2] Acts 2:42–47 [3] Frances Ridley Havergal, 1836–79

BIBLE IN A YEAR: **1 Samuel 25,26; Psalm 49**

In a Time of Crisis

Bring to God any national and international issues that concern you. Honestly acknowledge your hopes, confusions and fears about God's intervention in them.

The nation is in crisis, the result of a drought that affects all levels of society. For some, Jeremiah among them, this results in a crying out to God for his intervention: 'do something, LORD' (v 7), you are our 'hope' and our 'Saviour' (v 8). When nothing happens, scepticism breaks out. Is God merely a passer-by, is he confused, is he powerless? Others, desperate for a positive spin on the situation, listen to the self-deluded words of the prophets, the experts, the intellectuals. It appears that no one is prepared to listen to the genuine message from God, that they must face the consequences of their wilful breaking of the secure and stable covenant relationship with him.

There's nothing like a crisis to bring people to their knees. For the first time in the book of Jeremiah, there is what appears to be a genuine acknowledgement of their wickedness over a number of generations (v 20) and the futility of appealing to idols and foreign gods (v 22). If God does genuinely live among them (v 9), then he is the only source of hope (v 22). How sincere is this turnaround? How long will it last? Only time will tell.

These Bible notes were written in 2021 during the global pandemic. Some people, in desperation, turned to God. Others were more agnostic. Most hung on to the promises of politicians, scientists and analysts, only to be confused by contradictory advice and often disappointing results. Yet God never left home. He was immanent, present within and throughout our lives, in the darkness, the loss and the fear. He was and is the hope to which we cling, his presence, his power and his love demonstrated in 'Christ Jesus our hope'.[1]

Read 1 Peter 1:3–5. What does it mean for Jesus to give you 'a living hope'? Apply this to the reality of your present circumstances.

[1] 1 Tim 1:1

Jeremiah 15

The Luxury of Despair

Without wallowing, acknowledge before God the situations and issues that are getting you down.

The singer Martyn Joseph tells of his visit to a Palestinian refugee camp, the horror and anger he felt at the injustice of the situation and the inspiration he received from Abed, a children's theatre organiser, who carried on straining for peace and justice for his children because he couldn't afford 'the luxury of despair'.[1] Jeremiah would have echoed that sentiment.

In the face of a weary God, committed to subjecting Judah to endless punishments because he gave them every chance and they still spurned him, Jeremiah is on the verge of giving up. 'I've tried. What more can I do?' (see v 10). Then, in the midst of personal persecution and anguish, he tentatively reaches out to God: 'remember me and care for me' (v 15). Why? Because, like Judah at the start of the passage, he has to ask, 'Where shall we go?' (v 2). Judah goes to punishment. Jeremiah goes to the only one who can save and deliver (v 21) and he is not let down.

Peter gave a similar response to Jesus.[2] There was grumbling in the camp at the severity of Jesus' teaching. Many followers had left. When given that same option, Peter's reply was stark. Since he had met the Holy One of God, what other options were there? It wasn't a case of 'any port in a storm'. There was only one port worth berthing at.

It would be easy sometimes to despair at the state of the world in which we live, at breakdowns within our family and friendship relationships, at the wreckage of our personal lives. However, by turning again and again to God, there is the promise of restoration, protection and deliverance. It's the only way we have and the only one worth taking.

Physically turn yourself in a different direction. Use the new view as a stimulus for a period of praise and thankfulness to God for his faithfulness, especially in trying circumstances.

[1] Martyn's song 'The Luxury of Despair' can be found on his album *Sanctuary* [2] John 6:68,69

BIBLE IN A YEAR: 1 Samuel 29–31; 1 Corinthians 2

Singles and Doubles

Bring to God every member of your close family, praying for their protection and guidance in this day.

There is a deep and reciprocal love between me and my wife, my children and my grandchildren. That love both enriches me and makes demands on me in equal measure. Without it my life would be immeasurably impoverished. My heart goes out to Jeremiah when God tells him that he is not to marry or have children. Is this a symbolic act, or is the intention to free up Jeremiah in his service to God? In fact it appears to be something very different, a tender shielding of the prophet from the pain of the ensuing bereavement and loss that many in Judah will experience when plague, violence and famine devastate the land (vs 3,4). If he has no family, then he has no family to lose.

Singleness is not a popular option within many societies. Dating apps have multiplied, romcoms promise a happy ending in each other's arms, multiple short-term relationships are increasingly seen as normal. Yet Jesus, 'the author and finisher of our faith'[1] was single. Although he endorsed marriage[2] he acknowledged singleness as a significant option, sometimes because of circumstances but also, for some, to fulfil God's purposes.[3] The Greek word Paul uses to describe singleness in 1 Corinthians 7:7 is *charisma*. It is therefore a spiritual gift just as significant as healing, prophecy and tongues.

Single people within our churches have no less need of relationship than those of us who are privileged to be married. They have no less entitlement to the pleasure of a child's company, questioning and play. Hugs, birthday remembrances, a shoulder to cry on, gifts and celebrations are vital expressions of their value and purpose. Maybe your church, especially in its small groups, can become a surrogate family?

What does it feel like to be single? Ask someone. Open up a conversation that compares and contrasts.

[1] Heb 12:2, AV [2] Matt 19:4–6 [3] Matt 19:10–12

BIBLE IN A YEAR: **2 Samuel 1,2; Psalm 50**

The Simple Sabbath Test

Thank God for the challenge of his Word, both intellectual and spiritual.

It's been a rough road that we've travelled with Jeremiah. There have often been dark clouds overhead and signs of the impending storm. Only occasionally have there been glimpses of blue sky. Maybe, like me, you've come to admire the grace and courage of the prophet, his honest attempts to convey the words God has given him, despite disdain and open opposition. Sometimes I've empathised with him. Today's final day on the road gives us, first, an image that sums up the central issue (vs 5–8) and ends with a simple, practical test.

To flourish, a tree needs water. Similarly, to flourish, men and women need to trust in God. The shrub (barely worth calling a tree) in the parched land survives, but only just. The tree planted near the water source flourishes, even when conditions are hard. Jesus uses the same image,[1] with the living water of the Spirit not only flowing into us but also out to others, like fruit at harvest time.[2] The choice given to the kingdom of Judah is clear: where do you place your obedient trust, in yourselves or in God? Are you a flourishing fruit tree or a withered shrub?

A practical task is a reasonable way to test good intentions. So God asks the whole nation to comply with the requirements he gave regarding the Sabbath: on the one hand, to take a day off from work; on the other hand, to use the time to worship a holy God.[3] It's the simple choice that he's given throughout these chapters: is the nation for him or against him? Sadly, we suspect what the answer will be: a failed test and the inevitable judgement that will follow.

Give yourself the Sabbath test (the Sunday test in Christian terms):
Do you rest? What do you take a break from?
How do you make it holy to God?

[1] John 4:13,14; 7:37-39 [2] Gal 5:22,23 [3] Exod 20:8-11

BIBLE IN A YEAR: **2 Samuel 3-5; 1 Corinthians 3**

The Two Kings

Ask God for a clear and vibrant vision of the majesty of Jesus.

We find ourselves in a very different world from that of Jeremiah. We're transported into the scene of a royal wedding, a national event, throbbing with pageantry, enthusiasm and noise. The king is noble, skilful, excellent and mighty. He exudes splendour and majesty (vs 1–3). And just look at the bride's wedding dress (vs 13,14)! A match made in heaven. Yet the king isn't merely a poster boy for the monarchy. He also has responsibility for the moral, ethical and legal life of the nation. He is exhorted to fight for the cause of 'truth, humility and justice' (v 4). The future's looking good for a stable and prosperous reign.

Contrast this with a parallel event, the entry of Jesus into Jerusalem on the first Palm Sunday. There are crowds, but they're not marvelling at Jesus' handsome features, his military bearing or his sturdy mount. Nevertheless, the cry rings out:

'Blessed is the king who comes in the name of the Lord.'[1] Though gentle and humble in approach, his majesty shines through. Soon, in the city he will speak God's truth, he will humbly accept his fate and he will turn the injustice of a trumped-up trial and crucifixion into the triumph of the resurrection.

There are many pictures of Jesus but, unsurprisingly, no photographs. Each picture is therefore a personal interpretation. So how do you see him? If God is one of us, then how does he appear to you? How is he like you and me? How is he different? How does your picture of him influence your relationship with him? How does his majesty shine through for you? Do you feel the optimism and confidence in him that the crowd in the psalm obviously shared? Is the future looking good?

Use the words of the song 'Majesty, worship his majesty'[2] as stimulus for a period of personal worship.

---

[1] Luke 19:38 [2] Jack Hayford, 1981; there are many performances available on YouTube

BIBLE IN A YEAR: **2 Samuel 6,7; 1 Corinthians 4**

Jesus is Alive!

This Easter experience the amazing story of God's plan to save his people. Guardians of Ancora, developed by Scripture Union, is a free-to-download game that brings the stories of the Bible to life.

Experience the joy of knowing Jesus is alive and celebrate God's gift to all. Bring the story of the resurrection to life in the heart of a child this Easter. Download Guardians of Ancora for free and live the incredible adventures of Easter.

Download and play
Guardians of Ancora FOR FREE

 Find out more at guardiansofancora.com

JUSTICE AND HOPE

To many people, the Book of Revelation is a very strange book indeed. The kaleidoscope of images, the use of numbers, the strange structure – all of this can be very off-putting, making it a difficult read. As someone said in a different context, 'If you aren't confused, you don't really know what is going on!'

More strange, even, than the book itself is the way that many Christians read it and use it. It seems to me that we should read Revelation considering the issues that arise – as with reading any book of the Bible. That will involve looking at the context it was first written in and what kind of writing it is. Most of us are not familiar with the conventions of apocalyptic writing, but it is clear that the first followers of Jesus were quite at home with it: note the puzzled response of the disciples when Jesus uses parables,[1] yet their happy acceptance of his apocalyptic teaching![2] We will need to consider its place in the canon of Scripture – its use of the Old Testament and its parallels in the New. We must also attend carefully to the content – what does the text actually say?

The passages we are looking at involve some of the most challenging in the book – and perhaps the most challenging in the Bible. Yet all through, two themes stand out.

The first is God's justice. John appears to be aware that judgement raises questions. He includes various asides emphasising that God's judgements are just and that those who do not accept the free offer of the gift of life will find that their destiny reflects their decisions. The second is hope. Shining through the darkness of chaos and judgement is the light of the hope of the new creation that is to come, that God will one day be with his people – a hope that feeds and sustains us as we look to him.

Ian Paul

[1] Mark 4 [2] Mark 13

Revelation 12

Triumph and Testimony

Father, give me greater insight into the triumph 'by the blood of the Lamb'. As I live this out, grant me my own 'word of testimony'.[1]

This chapter presents us with a paradox. On the one hand, it is of central importance, written in a different style from the rest of the book. Instead of 'And I saw', John writes, 'A great sign appeared' (v 1), reverting to his usual language in the next chapter: he seems to want us to pay special attention to this sign. On the other hand, the structure, imagery and ideas seem baffling to the modern reader!

The central narrative is about a woman who gives birth, a dragon who threatens her, the woman being taken to safety and the child defeating and destroying the dragon. Anyone in the first century would immediately recognise this (it is the myth of Leto, Python and Apollo, in which Python threatened a pregnant Leto only to be killed by her child Apollo), not least because this story was deployed in imperial propaganda: the emperor becomes Apollo, who slays the monster Python, representing the forces of chaos and disorder. John, however, changes the story so that the dragon is the one who stands behind Roman power[2] and it is Jesus, not the emperor, who is the powerful ruler that ends chaos and brings peace.

John does this by inserting biblical characters into this pagan story: the suffering people of God,[3] images of Satan from across the Old Testament and the promised Messiah (v 5).[4] He also pauses the main story to add an explanation: Israel's angelic prince Michael has defeated Satan (v 9); and it is the sacrifice of Jesus ('the blood of the Lamb', v 11) that has defeated every power and freed us from condemnation.[5] It is only in Jesus that we find peace, security and forgiveness. Anyone else who claims to provide this is usurping the place of God and deceiving us.

What stories does my culture relate about itself? How does the gospel subvert these? How can we connect them with the story of what God has done in Jesus?

[1] Rev 12:11 [2] 'a beast coming out of the sea', Rev 13:1–8 [3] See Isa 66:7–9 [4] Ps 2:9 [5] Cf Rom 8:1

BIBLE IN A YEAR: **2 Samuel 8–10; 1 Corinthians 5**

Patient Endurance

'I pray that out of his glorious riches he may strengthen you with power through his Spirit in your inner being, so that Christ may dwell in your hearts.'[1]

John resumes his customary 'And I saw ...' to set out some terrifying images – not a vision of the future, but a revelation of the challenge of the present. The details of the first beast – its heads, horns, blasphemous names and conquest – are all drawn from the night vision of four beasts in Daniel 7. In Daniel, this pointed to the succession of empires ending with Rome, but John has combined this to depict an 'empire of empires' – a claim that Rome made for itself.

This very human power – symbolically arising from the 'sea' (v 1) of the nations in tumult, but literally coming across the Aegean to Asia – parodies the Lamb of chapter 5. Like the Lamb, it shares the throne and power of the one who sent it (v 2);[2] like the Lamb, it has recovered from an apparently fatal wound; it makes people acclaim the power behind its throne in terms that belong to God. 'Who is like the beast?' (v 4) echoes the claim of God's incomparability;[3] 'Who is like God?' is the meaning of the name Michael (*mi*, who, *ca*, is like, *el*, God).

This presents a real challenge for John's readers, both then and now. Such empires in history frequently blaspheme by demanding the loyalty that belongs only to God. The followers of the Lamb, who refuse to compromise, suffer and appear to be conquered (v 7) – yet there is hope. The 42 months of oppression are also a time for bearing witness (calculated as 1,260 days)[4] and a time of protection and nourishing by God.[5] The words 'was given' (vs 5,7) point to the higher authority of God. The beast's 'authority over every tribe, people, language and nation' (v 7) is still subject to Jesus' rule[6] and his redemption.[7]

How can I discern where 'the powers that be'[8] are claiming loyalty that belongs only to God? What does it mean to live with 'patient endurance'[9] in Jesus?

---

[1] Eph 3:16,17 [2] Cf Rev 5:13 [3] Cf Exod 15:11 [4] See Rev 11:2,3 [5] Rev 12:6,14 [6] Rev 1:5 [7] Rev 5:9 [8] Rom 13:1, AV [9] Rev 1:9

BIBLE IN A YEAR: **2 Samuel 11,12; Psalm 51**

The Beast and his Number

'I am your servant; give me understanding, that I may know your testimonies!'[1]

Today's passage includes what must be the most notorious verse in the Bible, the number of the beast in verse 18. To make sense of it, we need to notice three things.

First, in the ancient world with no separate number system, letters had a numerical value and it was common to calculate the value of phrases and sayings. There are inscriptions in Pompeii, Ephesus, Smyrna and other cities where we find things like 'I love her whose number is 545'; it is easy to calculate the number of someone's name, but very difficult to do the reverse calculation, so this would only be understood by those in the know. Often the calculation was done in another language, since many were multilingual in Greek, Latin and a local language. Second, the mark of the beast (vs 17,18) forms a pair with the 'seal on the foreheads of the servants of our God'.[2]

Those who follow the beast carry its mark – and this results in final judgement[3] – but those who follow the Lamb receive his seal (which turns out to be the name of the Lamb and his Father)[4] and are protected and saved. No one expects the seal to be visible, so why should we expect the 'mark' to be?

Third, both the word 'beast' and the name 'Nero Caesar' have the value 666 when the Greek words are written in Hebrew letters.[5] Early readers clearly knew this; the variant 616 found in Bible footnotes is the value when 'Nero' is spelt differently. John is telling his readers: the everyday activities of buying and selling, leisure and entertainment are not neutral but involve us making decisions. You cannot follow the Lamb and simply follow the dominant culture: you have to make a choice.

How do my everyday decisions – buying and selling, how I spend my time, where I find entertainment, the use of technology – reflect my faith? Do my habits need to change?

[1] Ps 119:125, ESV [2] Rev 7:3 [3] Rev 14:11 [4] Rev 14:1 [5] The word 'angel' in Rev 21:17 adds up to 144

BIBLE IN A YEAR: **2 Samuel 13,14; 1 Corinthians 6**

A Purified People of Hope

'We always thank God for ... your work produced by faith, your labour prompted by love, and your endurance inspired by hope in our Lord Jesus Christ.'[1]

If the previous chapter offered a stark picture from an earthly point of view, then this section offers, as a counterpoint, an uplifting one from a heavenly perspective. It tells us about the followers of the Lamb – where they are, what they are doing and what they are like. They 'stand on Mount Zion' (v 1), which in the Old Testament is another way of talking about the Temple in Jerusalem, the place of God's presence. That is why those whom the first beast blasphemes are described as 'those who live in heaven'.[2] As Paul puts it, he has 'seated us with him in the heavenly realms in Christ Jesus'.[3]

The '144,000' (v 1) are those whom John hears about[4] and when he turns to see them they are 'a great multitude that no one could count, from every nation, tribe, people and language',[5] who have been described as 'redeemed' for God by the Lamb,[6] the language repeated here (v 3). Their harps have become part of the popular cliché about heaven – but in fact they are the instruments of the Levitical priests in Temple worship.[7] This is a priestly people,[8] who sing the song of God's gracious redemption to the whole world[9] and who therefore sound like God himself ('many waters'[10]) – these saints are singing from the same hymn-sheet as Jesus.

The phrase 'did not defile themselves with women, for they remained virgins' (v 4) is metaphorical. It draws on the Old Testament metaphor of sexual purity symbolising devotion to God and the rejection of idolatry, so that God's people become the 'bride' of Christ.[11] The seven qualities become a sign of hope ('firstfruits', v 4) to the world.

Identify areas of your life, in thought, speech or action, where you should open yourself to the Spirit's purifying power. How can you be a better sign of hope?

[1] 1 Thess 1:2,3 [2] Rev 13:6 [3] Eph 2:6 [4] Rev 7:4 [5] Rev 7:9 [6] Rev 5:9, AV [7] 1 Chr 15:16 [8] Rev 1:6 [9] Ps 96:1,2 [10] Rev 1:15, AV [11] Rev 19:7

BIBLE IN A YEAR: **2 Samuel 15,16; 1 Corinthians 7**

Revelation 14:6–20

Judgement and Hope

'The steadfast love of the LORD never ceases; his mercies never come to an end; they are new every morning; great is your faithfulness.'[1]

The startling images of judgement here draw on earlier images in the book and anticipate the scenes of judgement coming later. We need to note three things to read this well and make sense of it.

First, the phrase 'tormented with burning sulphur' (v 10) seems gruesome to the modern ear and has led some to believe in God's judgement as 'eternal conscious torment'. However, 'the smoke of their torment will rise for ever and ever' (v 11) parallels the similar phrase about Babylon.[2] Both come from Old Testament images of the destruction.[3] A city cannot be continually destroyed; the point about the smoke rising for ever and ever is that the destruction is final; the focus is not on the *process* of judgement, but its *result*. Second, the strange phrase 'the maddening wine' (v 8) is an exact

parallel to the 'wine of God's fury' (v 10), though English translations obscure this. So, John is saying, if you allow yourself to be seduced by the lies of Babylon, you will get what you deserve. This is another way of saying 'People reap what they sow'[4] or, as Paul expresses it, God gives people over to the consequences of their decisions[5] – as part of giving us real responsibility for our actions. Third, the message of judgement is bracketed with good news. It is introduced with the announcement of the 'eternal gospel' by an angel 'flying in mid-air' (v 6) – that is, in a place where all can see and hear the invitation – and ends with the 'rest' (v 13) that is found only in Jesus. The last word of Revelation is a word of hope: 'let all who wish take the free gift of the water of life'.[6]

How does the message of God's just judgement offer hope to the oppressed and those who have been abused? Where do I need to find this hope in my life?

[1] Lam 3:22,23, ESV [2] Rev 18:9,18 [3] Isa 34:10 [4] Gal 6:7, TNIV; cf Hos 8:7 [5] Rom 1:24 [6] Rev 22:17, TNIV

BIBLE IN A YEAR: **2 Samuel 17,18; Psalms 52–54**

Disclosure and Mystery

'For his anger lasts only a moment, but his favour lasts a lifetime; weeping may remain for a night, but rejoicing comes in the morning.'[1]

Each of the three sequences (seals, trumpets, bowls) provides a structured framework for the apparent chaos of the world, from the present to the end, pointing to God's ultimate sovereignty. God remains at arm's length, acting through intermediaries; the chaos is not beyond his control, but his personal word is of healing and peace.[2]

The previous sequences raised a question – what is God going to do about the world? – and the interlude between the sixth and seventh elements in each sequence offered an answer: he will form a prophetic people to be faithful witnesses to God and the Lamb. This sequence is different: instead of interludes in the middle, we have an introduction at the beginning, which provides a context for what follows by reminding us of earlier scenes in the book and earlier episodes in the story of God's people.

We are reminded of the 'sign ... in heaven':[3] the woman, who represents God's oppressed people, waiting for deliverance through Jesus. We are reminded of the 'sea of glass' before the throne,[4] itself a reminder of the bronze laver before the first Temple[5] and the encounter of Moses with God on Sinai.[6] The seven messages in chapters 2 and 3 each ended with a call to conquer, a victory over the beast[7] that has come through the blood of the Lamb.[8] The song of Moses and the Lamb (v 3) takes us back to the 144,000 on Mount Zion, and also draws on the songs of Moses;[9] Jesus leads us on a new Exodus journey, from sin to the new Jerusalem. The time of wrath and chaos will come to an end: God's action in the world might be hidden by the smoke of his glory, but we shall one day see him face to face.[10]

Scripture provides a context for making sense of challenges involved in following Jesus. What do you need to understand now – and what can you take on trust?

---

[1] Ps 30:5, TNIV [2] Rev 21:5 [3] Rev 12:1 [4] Rev 4:6 [5] 1 Kings 7:23 [6] Exod 24:10 [7] Rev 13:1 [8] Rev 12:11 [9] Exod 15; Deut 32 [10] Rev 22:4

BIBLE IN A YEAR: **2 Samuel 19,20; 1 Corinthians 8**

Psalm 46

Strength and Refuge

'Christ with me, Christ before me, Christ behind me, Christ within me, Christ beneath me, Christ above me, Christ at my right, Christ at my left'.[1]

This well-known psalm has been set to music in several languages. It is full of vivid images and offers a deep sense of assurance of the power and protection of God. Most readers don't have any difficulty with the images here – but they are not far removed from the apocalyptic language we have been immersed in this week!

Looking around us, it seems at times as though the earth gives way (v 2), reminding us of the mountains and islands in flight.[2] Then again, something like a mountain 'was thrown into the sea'[3] and in Daniel's vision the winds churned up the great sea, from which the beasts emerged.[4] We find earthquakes here in verse 3 and throughout Revelation. God's judgement against the warring nations comes with fire in verse 9, a major symbol of final judgement in the last third of

Revelation. When we are unsettled or puzzled by the images in Revelation, it is worth noting that this language is used all through Scripture.

The answer to the uncertainty around us is presented with two contrasting elements. On the one hand, the refuge God offers is found in a very specific place: the 'city of God' and the 'holy place' (v 4) refer to Jerusalem at the heart of Israel, the Temple within it and the Holy of Holies at the centre. The God who is a fortress is the 'God of Jacob' (v 7) and none other. And yet, on the other hand, this God will be 'exalted among the nations' (v 10) and will do his work 'to the ends of the earth' (v 9). The God of Scripture is a God of the particular and the universal; he is the God of Israel, whose grace, peace and power have now, through Jesus, been made available to all.

At what points in life do I feel insecure and need to look to God as my fortress? Who around me needs to discover this truth?

[1] Patrick's Breastplate [2] Rev 6:14; 16:20 [3] Rev 8:8 [4] Dan 7:2,3

BIBLE IN A YEAR: **2 Samuel 21,22; 1 Corinthians 9**

Judgements Just and True

'He is the Rock, his works are perfect, and all his ways are just. A faithful God who does no wrong, upright and just is he.'[1]

In this chapter, we are further plunged into some of the most challenging images of judgement in the Bible. This is not a prediction of future vindictive acts by an angry deity; we have seen earlier in the book that John appears to be describing the world he is living in, not a future apocalyptic age. There is no reason to think these are literal: they are not literally possible, and we have been happy to recognise the symbolic meaning of the other images in the book.

We also need to recognise that the language here closely matches two other descriptions of God's judgement in the Bible. The first is the ten plagues that come on the nation of Egypt,[2] which God sends in response to Pharoah's refusal to 'Let my people go'.[3] We thus find mention of blood, hail, boils, darkness and frogs, all from the Exodus account, and it is this close correspondence which makes this sequence different from the seals and the trumpets. The other parallel is with the teaching of Jesus. The language of gnawing their tongues and cursing in verses 10 and 11 comes very close to Jesus' repeated mention in Matthew's Gospel of 'outer darkness', where there is 'weeping and gnashing of teeth'.[4]

Central to this sequence is the interlude in verses 5–7; it is almost as if the agents involved anticipate our objections and pause the action to offer a commentary. The central principle of God's judgements is that they are 'true and just ' (v 7); God is giving to people what they have given to others (the principle of *lex talionis*) and is following the consequences of what they have chosen. If we interpret God's judgements in any other way, we have missed the point.

Do I struggle with the idea of God acting with this kind of justice? Why (not)? To whom in the world today will this teaching be important?

[1] Deut 32:4 [2] Exod 7–11 [3] Exod 5:1 [4] Matt 8:12; 22:13; 25:30, AV

BIBLE IN A YEAR: **2 Samuel 23,24; 1 Corinthians 10**

Revelation 16:12–21

Dressed and Ready

'Nothing in my hands I bring, / simply to thy cross I cling; / naked, come to thee for dress ... foul, I to the fountain fly, / wash me, Saviour, or I die.'[1]

This chapter concludes the structured, cosmic overview of history that began in chapter 6; soon we will turn to the specific fate of Rome as the archetypal human empire, before the seven visions of the end running from 19:11 to 22:7. Despite their place here, these verses have been commandeered into end-times timetables, because of the specific mention of the Euphrates (v 12) and Armageddon (v 16).

These were real places for John's readers – but each had a symbolic significance. The Euphrates traditionally marked the eastern boundary of the empire, so 'kings from the East' (v 12) signify the Parthians and others, coming to destroy the apparent peace and order of Roman rule. Rome is not, despite its claims, the 'eternal city', and one day its false promise of security will be shown for what it is. Armageddon, in Hebrew *Har* ('hill of') *Megiddo*, was a Canaanite fortress on the south side of the plain of Jezreel, which had been the site of important battles.[2] It thus became proverbial for decisive conflicts that would bring kingdoms to an end – and it has recovered its proverbial sense in popular culture today. No human empire can withstand the coming of God in power – the awesome majesty of God is such that even the created world (islands and mountains, v 20) cannot stand in his presence.

How should we prepare for this end? Once more, there is a verbal intervention (v 15) – this time, the words of Jesus himself, steering us away from all end-times calculations. He will come at a moment no one expects or can predict ('like a thief in the night'[3]); the only way to be ready is to be found in Christ, clothed with the good deeds that come from faithful obedience.

How well dressed are you in 'compassion, kindness, humility, gentleness and patience'?[4] Is there anger, selfishness or jealously in your life that needs to be addressed?

[1] AM Toplady, 1740–78, 'Rock of Ages' [2] Judg 1:27; 5:19; 1 Kings 9:15 [3] 1 Thess 5:2 [4] Col 3:12

BIBLE IN A YEAR: **1 Kings 1,2; Psalm 55**

Resisting Seduction

'Be alert and of sober mind. Your enemy the devil prowls around like a roaring lion looking for someone to devour. Resist him, standing firm.'[1]

As we enter the final sections of Revelation, there are some striking changes. John is accompanied for the first time by an interpreting angel, who explains what he sees in a way similar to Jewish apocalypses.[2] That means that John now (until 19:10) is mostly recording what he *hears*, rather than what he *sees*; nearly half of Revelation is speech report rather than a vision. The major element of the vision – the woman riding on a scarlet beast in the desert – describes Roman imperial power in quite different terms from before.

There is a powerful contrast between the city-woman Babylon and the city-woman the new Jerusalem, both of whom are shown to John by 'One of the seven angels' of the bowls (v 1).[3] The first sits in the desert, depends on the ultimately destructive power of the beast, is adorned with luxury gained from oppression and will meet an untimely end. The second rests on a high mountain, is sustained by the life-giving power of God, is adorned by the gifts of grace and will endure for ever. John's audience is therefore presented with a powerful rhetorical challenge: to which of these city-women will they give their allegiance? In which is found their true citizenship?

The king lists in verses 10–12 have been used in various ways to date the book of Revelation – but that cannot have been John's intention, since he and his contemporaries knew when he was writing! Their symbolism points to the reality of human empires and those seduced by them: they will not last, and, rather than giving people dignity and freedom, they debase and humiliate them. It is a path that leads to death and destruction.

Where in your culture and context do you sense the seductive pull of a life that draws you away from the spiritual disciplines of peace, contentment and simplicity?

[1] 1 Pet 5:8,9 [2] Eg 4 Ezra (part of 2 Esdras, in the Apocrypha) [3] Rev 21:9

BIBLE IN A YEAR: **1 Kings 3–5; 1 Corinthians 11**

Worship and Wealth

'Create in me a pure heart, O God, and renew a steadfast spirit within me ... grant me a willing spirit, to sustain me.'[1]

Throughout this chapter, John continues mostly to hear rather than see things. The opening proclamation is remarkable – it sees the judgement of God over the empire as so certain that it declares it as having already happened, in the past tense. Equally striking is the description of the angel who makes this announcement – 'He had great authority, and the earth was illuminated by his splendour' (v 1). The judgement of exploitative imperial power is depicted as good news for the whole world.

What is rather surprising, though, is the nature of the sin for which Rome is denounced. We might have thought that idolatry – giving to the emperor the praise and loyalty that is due to God alone – would be the main issue. That is the focus of earlier chapters, where the language of worship in heaven borrows from the imperial cult and gives to God the honours of the emperor. We might also think that sexual immorality is a concern, as in other parts of the New Testament, not least because the Judeo-Christian ethic of relationships was so at odds with the pagan world. When we read the three accusations in verse 3 in parallel, however, we can see that the main focus is the seductive temptation of wealth and power.

The immorality of the kings of the earth involved 'luxury' (v 9); kings across the empire saw their own power enhanced by the relationship with Rome, and that often allowed the accrual of great wealth. The 'merchants of the earth grew rich' (v 3), reflecting the importance of trade to keep the empire running. John, borrowing language from Jeremiah 51:45 calling God's exiled people from the literal Babylon, urges his readers to separate themselves from this way of life and live by a different set of values.

In a consumer culture, where we are told that buying things is the answer to our problems, how easy is it to live differently and distinctively?

[1] Ps 51:10,12

BIBLE IN A YEAR: 1 Kings 6,7; 1 Corinthians 12

The Litmus Test of Wealth

'Do not worry, saying, "What shall we eat?" … or "What shall we wear?" … seek first his kingdom and his righteousness, and all these things will be given to you.'[1]

John continues to describe the voices he hears – but in a distinctive, structured way. Three groups repeat a double cry of 'Woe! Woe …' (vs 10,16,19), the kings of the earth, the merchants and the sea captains, all of whom have enriched themselves by their consorting with Rome. The main focus, however, is on the merchants. The theme of ostentatious wealth is prominent throughout: 'luxury and splendour' (v 14); 'gained their wealth' (vs 15,19); 'fine linen, purple and scarlet, and glittering with gold, precious stones and pearls' (v 16).

John spells this out in two ways. First, he is specific about the nature of the wealth and the impact of its accumulation. The list of cargoes in verses 11–13 reads like a tour around a luxury house in first-century Rome; the word for 'carriage' (*rheda*, v 13) refers to a particular four-wheeled carriage used by better-off Romans; pearls (v 12) were so prized that the richest would dissolve them in vinegar and drink them with wine to demonstrate their wealth. 'Purple' and 'scarlet' refer to the expensive fabrics made from crushed shells that only the elite could wear.

Second, John expresses the critique of wealth in biblical and theological language. The list of 28 cargoes here is adapted from the list of 40 cargoes cited in the judgement of Tyre in Ezekiel 27; the sins of this empire are the same sins that have always beset people who turn from God to material things for security and fulfilment. The loss of their wealth 'never to be recovered' (v 14) echoes Satan's expulsion from heaven: 'they lost their place in heaven'.[2] The contrast between 'woe' and 'rejoice' (vs 19,20) echoes the responses to Satan's fall.[3] How we handle wealth and power is a test and reflection of our spiritual state.

When you came to faith, how did your attitude to wealth and possessions change? How has it developed as your faith has grown and matured?

[1] Matt 6:31,33 [2] Rev 12:8 [3] Rev 12:12

BIBLE IN A YEAR: **1 Kings 8,9; Psalms 56,57**

Revelation 19:1–10

Praise for What's to Come

'... being confident of this, that he who began a good work in you will carry it on to completion until the day of Christ Jesus.'[1]

This section starting at 17:1 depicting the fall of Babylon – for John, this is Rome, but portrayed as the archetype of exploitative human empires through history – ends with a cascade of praise. The previous threefold 'woe' contrasts with threefold 'rejoicing' here. The central anthem comes from the elders and living creatures we met in chapter 4, but on either side we hear from 'a great multitude' (vs 1,6), not only of the myriad angels but also the redeemed, whom no one can count.[2] They now sound like 'the roar of rushing waters' and 'loud peals of thunder' – the first of which may be compared to the voice of God.[3] It seems as though the people of God are in harmony not only with the creation of God but also with the voice of God in the presence of God.

It is commonly said that praise is the language of heaven and that the worship we practise now is a rehearsal for spending eternity with God, but there are no hymns of praise in the next vision, of the new Jerusalem; this is the last hymn-like material in the book. Praise is not simply for what God has done or what he is doing, but for what he is going to do when his justice is fully revealed at the end. The praise here, though expressed in the past tense since in the narrative it follows the account of Babylon's fall, is for John's readers still anticipating something in the future.

Even John, though, after his extraordinary visions and privileged access to the presence of God, is still liable to error and sin, and has to be rebuked by the angel. We need to praise God, to remember where we are heading, even as we continue on the journey.

In what aspect of your life and faith have you seen growth and maturity? Where do you still need help? How does praise assist in that growth?

---

[1] Phil 1:6 [2] Rev 7:9 [3] Ezek 1:24

BIBLE IN A YEAR: **1 Kings 10,11; 1 Corinthians 13**

Psalm 47

God is For Us

'God's love has been poured out into our hearts through the Holy Spirit.'[1] Invite God to do this again today.

This is another psalm of exuberant praise – which has also been set to music in different contexts. Like Psalm 46, it has a focus on the particular and the universal. The God we praise is the Lord, the particular God of the nation of Israel; whenever we see LORD (in small capitals, vs 2,5) that is a translation of his name, which was thought too holy actually to say. He is the pride of Jacob and the God of Abraham – but we need to note why we should praise him and who is invited to the praise party.

At first it might read like a nationalistic celebration: 'He subdued nations under us' (v 3). At first it seems as though he is the God of Israel, but *not* the God of the Egyptians, the Canaanites or the Edomites. However, there is something more nuanced going on here: 'He chose our inheritance for us ... whom he loved' (v 4). God has set his love on Israel, not because they are great, or because they deserve it, but just because he has.[2] Our natural response to thinking about the greatness of God is to think of ourselves as small – but the psalmist does the opposite, because he is so convinced that this great God is on his side. God's power *for us* is something to shout about.

This God of Israel is also the God of all nations. He reigns over the 'kings of the earth' (v 9), a phrase Revelation picks up in declaring that Jesus is 'ruler of the kings of the earth'.[3] The celebration of God being 'for us' (v 4) isn't in any sense 'He is on my side, so he is against you', but 'God is for me – and you can discover that he is for you as well'.

In the different contexts of your daily life – home, work, school, neighbourhood – what might it mean to realise that 'God is for me'?

[1] Rom 5:5 [2] See Deut 7:7,8 [3] Rev 1:5

BIBLE IN A YEAR: **1 Kings 12,13; 1 Corinthians 14**

Revelation 19:11–21

The Battle That is Not

**'... thanks be to God! He gives us the victory through our Lord Jesus Christ.'[1]
Praise God that he has already conquered in Jesus.**

This is the beginning of a significant new section (the chapter divisions are misleading), marked by the unique phrase 'I saw heaven standing open' (v 1). Earlier, John went through an open door;[2] now heaven itself is opened and is finally united with the earth. This is what we long for when we pray 'Your kingdom come ... on earth as in heaven'. Revelation is a sequence of visions, rather than a vision of a sequence of events, so there is no need to read an end-times chronology here. Rather, we have seven unnumbered visions, each beginning 'I saw'.[3] These visions don't point to different *stages* of Jesus' return, but to different *aspects* of what it means.

In the first vision, Jesus is contrasted sharply with the first horseman in chapter 6. Rather than conquering for gain, by might, Jesus comes as 'king of kings and lord of lords' (see v 16) by right, the one who is entitled to rule since he shares the throne of God. His weapon is not an actual sword, but the sword from his mouth, which is the word of God's truth. He comes to rule with justice and righteousness.

In the second vision we have the bizarre image of birds gorging on flesh (vs 18,21), which makes no sense (not least because the kings who are consumed reappear in the new Jerusalem[4]) until we realise that this language comes from Ezekiel 39:17, where it is a picture of God liberating his people from all oppression. In the third vision, there is a battle – which isn't a battle! There is no description of struggle, because the victory was already won on the cross.[5] Now, not only is evil defeated, but its origins (the beast and the false prophet) are destroyed.

Think of an area of your life where you are aware of struggle and conflict. How might you see that differently knowing that Jesus has already won the victory?

---

[1] 1 Cor 15:57 [2] Rev 4:1,2 [3] Rev 19;11,17,19; 20:1,4,11; 21:1 [4] Rev 21:24 [5] Rev 12:10

BIBLE IN A YEAR: **1 Kings 14,15; 1 Corinthians 15**

Eternal Weight of Glory

'I pray ... that you may know the hope to which he has called you, the riches of his glorious inheritance.'[1]

We come to the fourth and (start of the) fifth visions ('And I saw ...', vs 1,4), over which much theological ink has been spilled! The meaning of 'a thousand years' (v 2) has been debated since the second century, but several things are evident.

First, John never uses numbers literally; they are always symbolic. The seven churches[2] were not the only seven; the number stands for 'the whole church', which is why they hear each other's messages and we overhear them all. A thousand years symbolises a long period, which is why many human empires claim they will last 'a thousand years' (they rarely do). This period of Satan's defeat and the reign of the saints is vast in comparison with the short time of three and a half years of tribulation and testing. 'For our light and momentary troubles are achieving for us an eternal glory that far outweighs them all.'[3]

Within Revelation, a thousand has an additional meaning. As 10 cubed (10^3) it symbolises God's holy presence, since the Holy of Holies was cube-shaped. Thus the saints are numbered as a square times a cube[4] and the holy city is a cube cubed![5] This makes it very difficult to think that the thousand years stand for the 'church age', as if all is right with the world now, before Jesus returns. In our world, where everything is locked, keys mean access, but in the ancient world locks were rare and keys meant security. In the age to come, the world will be completely secure from Satan's influence – and those who 'did not love their lives so much as to shrink from death'[6] will be vindicated *on earth* as they reign with Jesus. Whatever trouble we face now, as we follow him, we will be more than rewarded.

What most frustrates you in your spiritual life and the world around you? How might you grow in the 'patient endurance'[7] that we all need to learn?

[1] Eph 1:18 [2] Rev 1–3 [3] 2 Cor 4:17 [4] Rev 7:4 [5] Rev 21:16 [6] Rev 12:11 [7] Rev 1:9

BIBLE IN A YEAR: **1 Kings 16,17; Psalms 58,59**

Revelation 20:7–15

Victory and Judgement

'Create in me a pure heart … Then I will teach transgressors your ways … Open my lips, Lord, and my mouth will declare your praise.'[1]

This fifth vision is one of the most debated and obscure in the book. John uses imagery from Ezekiel 38 and 39, reworking it freely. In Ezekiel, Gog rules over Magog, but here they are two nations; there, the scene of birds feasting on flesh follows the battle; here the order is reversed. The 'camp of God's people' (v 9) recalls the Exodus wanderings, even though the saints have just been reigning; the mention of 'the city he loves' (v 9) looks ahead to the new Jerusalem of the next chapter. As someone said, 'If you are not confused, you don't know what is going on!'

Yet we can still learn from this text. Once more, God's victory is instantaneous and without human effort; the 'fire … from heaven' (v 9) reminds us of Elijah.[2] Despite the overwhelming odds – their number is 'like the sand on the seashore' (v 8) – there is no doubt about the outcome; God and Satan are not equal powers. The imperial systems that were Satan's instruments (the beast and the false prophet) have been destroyed; now the power behind the throne of oppression shares their fate.

In the sixth of these seven visions, God takes his throne to enact judgement over all the world. Through the two (sets of) books (the books of the deeds and the Lamb's book of life) there is a focus on grace amidst judgement, on the free offer of life in the midst of accountability for how we have lived. God is supreme; when the sea, and 'death' and 'Hades' (v 13), the traditional abodes of the dead, have given up their inhabitants, they too are destroyed in 'the lake of fire' (v 14). Not just the causes, but the consequences of sin and evil are done away with.

Which am I most aware of – God's grace to me, or the responsibility that he calls me to in living for him? How do these relate to one another?

---

[1] Ps 51:10,13,15 [2] 1 Kings 18, alluded to in Rev 11:5

BIBLE IN A YEAR: **1 Kings 18,19; 1 Corinthians 16**

Invitation and Decision

'... if anyone is in Christ, the new creation has come.'[1] Ask God to renew his work in you today.

The final of these seven unnumbered visions – and the closing vision of the book – is one of dazzling splendour. All the themes of Revelation are drawn together here; indeed, there are numerous ideas gathered from all over Scripture. It really is a fitting end to the book and to the whole canon of Scripture.

Key to understanding this vision is noticing the direction of travel: the New Jerusalem, the dwelling place of God with his people, comes down from heaven to earth. Thus the realms that were separated at creation are finally reunited. It is apt that the city-people of God are described as the bride of Jesus, the Lamb, who is the groom (imagery we also find in the Gospels[2]). God came to his people in the incarnation of Jesus and his presence continued with the gift of the Spirit, but now the fullness of God's presence dwells

in intimate relationship with his people; the first words spoken in this book by the one seated on the throne come right at the end, as there is no more need of intermediaries – and his words are words of comfort and love.

As throughout the book, gracious invitation and exhortation to decision sit side by side. The invitation is to drink 'without cost from the spring of the water of life' (v 6) – all are included in the gracious offer of God. Yet the city is holy, which means that all sin is excluded; the decision to drink is the decision to leave sin behind. The new thing that God is doing is in continuity with all that has gone before: the city gates carry the names of the tribes of the first covenant, while the foundations carry the names of the apostles of the second.

What new thing is God doing in your life just now? How is that in continuity with what went before? What new dimension is it bringing?

---

[1] 2 Cor 5:17 [2] Matt 9:15

BIBLE IN A YEAR: 1 Kings 20,21; 2 Corinthians 1

Revelation 21:15–27

The Richness of Intimacy

'I pray that you, being rooted and established in love, may have power ... to grasp how wide and long and high and deep is the love of Christ.'[1]

In the details of the city, John is doing his theology by architecture. The Holy of Holies in the Jerusalem Temple was a cube, symbolising the holy perfection of God, and the new Jerusalem is a vast cube. This is the Holy of Holies, but on a colossal scale, stretching (if centred on Patmos) from Rome in the east to Jerusalem in the west. It is the perfect counterpoint to that archetype of imperial oppression, Rome: the value of the letters of 'Nero Caesar' when written in Hebrew is 666; the value of 'angel' is 144.

The gemstones make the city, the bride of the Lamb, a counterpoint to the harlot's 'precious stones' in chapter 17. The list here draws from both the gems representing the twelve tribes on Aaron's breast-piece[2] and the treasure of the king of Tyre.[3] Whatever worldly wealth is gained by greed and exploitation pales into insignificance in comparison with the riches of being the people of God by the gift of his grace.

Given all the allusions to the Old Testament, especially to Ezekiel, it comes as a great surprise that there is no Temple. The Temple signifies the meeting point of heaven and earth, the limited presence of God in the world – but now the whole city is filled with God's presence as heaven and earth unite. The space occupied by the presence of God is the same space occupied by the people of God – here is God in an intimacy with his people that has no limit. Remarkably, the 'kings of the earth' and the 'nations' (v 24), who have previously been the enemies of God, are able to share in this privilege.

In what ways have you experienced intimacy with God as a treasure beyond price? How might you grow in that sense of intimacy and its value?

[1] Eph 3:17,18 [2] Exod 28 [3] Ezek 28

BIBLE IN A YEAR: **1 Kings 22;** Psalms 60,61

Streams of Living Water

'Give me once more this water of life, that I will never again be thirsty.'[1]

This is the first time within John's tour that he makes explicit mention of 'the throne', the singular seat of 'God and of the Lamb' (v 1); Jesus and the Father share their unhindered reign of grace and life over the whole city. Where the visions of the throne-room of God became ever more complex and cluttered in earlier chapters, here is direct focus on the reign of God.

The 'river of the water of life' that flows from it has many antecedents in scripture – the stream that gives life to the righteous in Psalm 1, the streams of renewed Zion in Isaiah 33:21, the stream flowing from the Temple in Ezekiel 47. This river represents not merely what God gives, but the gift of God himself;[2] in the absence of any other mention, this must surely be a symbol of the Spirit of God who brings life to his people.

The servants of God in the city are the very ones for whom this vision and auditory message were given in the first place.[3] They were marked with the 'seal of the living God',[4] which is 'his [the Lamb's] name and his Father's name'[5] and the counterbalance to the mark of the beast.[6] As they perform priestly duties in this giant, cube-shaped holy of holies in God's holy presence, having God's name on their forehead makes them look, not just like a kingdom of priests (which was God's intention from the beginning[7]) but like Aaron himself.[8] We are not there yet; even John is prone to error, mistakenly worshipping the angel; like us, he is on a journey to perfection. This vision, however, gives us hope of a wonderful future.

What helps you to grow in excitement at the future that God has for his people? What helps you grow in patience as you journey towards it?

[1] Modified from John 4:15 [2] Cf Jer 2:13 [3] Rev 1:1 [4] Rev 7:2 [5] Rev 14:1 [6] Rev 13:16–18 [7] Exod 19:6; Rev 1:6 [8] Exod 28:36

BIBLE IN A YEAR: **2 Kings 1–3; 2 Corinthians 2**

Psalm 48

Extravagant Praise

Invite the Spirit of God to fill your heart once again with the praise of God. 'Open my lips, Lord, and my mouth will declare your praise.'[1]

This psalm invites us to revel in the protection and provision of God. The opening and closing sections reflect on the beauty of what God has done for and among his people, expressed in extravagant terms – Zion (Jerusalem) is breathtaking in its beauty, its elevation over the coastal plains, its fortifications. When we encounter the wonder of what God has done, there is sometimes nothing more to be done than to drink it in.

The central section gives us reasons for this wonder – and, as with the preceding psalms, there is a powerful mix of nationalism and universalism. It is clear that this is the God of Israel, the Lord; he is a warrior for Israel as the 'LORD of hosts' (v 8, AV), the armies of Israel; and he has utterly defeated the enemies of Israel. Yet this is not a naked exercise of power – it comes from God's nature as someone who is characterised by his steadfast love and kindness to Israel (the term *hesed*, 'steadfast' or 'unfailing' love in v 9). It comes, too, from his justice and righteousness; the term *tsedeq* in verse 10 is used to describe scales that weigh accurately and fairly. God defends Israel not out of bias, but out of a commitment to fairness, defending the weak against the strong.

We now read this psalm with a new perspective. God's praise 'reaches to the ends of the earth' (v 10) because people from every tribe, language, people and nation have been grafted into his people.[2] His righteousness has led to the offer of life to all people.[3] Our enemies are not flesh and blood;[4] the city and Temple in which we praise God is the body of believers in Jesus, whose praise will reach perfection in the new Jerusalem.

What have you recently learnt about God that causes your heart to sing? How might you express that in praise for yourself – and for others to join in?

[1] Ps 51:15 [2] Rev 7:9 [3] Rom 3:22 [4] Eph 6:12

BIBLE IN A YEAR: **2 Kings 4,5; 2 Corinthians 3**

Revelation 22:10–21

The Coming of Jesus

'I consider that our present sufferings are not worth comparing with the glory that will be revealed in us.'[1] Praise God for this hope.

We now confront the final paradox of Revelation: we have reached the end of the book, but the end has not yet come. Does that mean that this text is about a distant future for John and his contemporaries, a prediction of the end-times in our own day? Emphatically not! The command 'Do not seal up the words ...' (v 10) contradicts the message to Daniel,[2] whose visions in the sixth-century BC related to the distant, second-century BC reality. John's message was for John's readers in John's day; the hope that Jesus would soon come was to sustain them in faithful living, not turn them into end-times speculators.

There are two complementary movements emphasised throughout. The major one is the longing for Jesus to 'Come' (v 20). This is Jesus' promise; this is the desire of his people (the 'bride', v 17); this is the yearning of the Spirit. Why?

Because the coming of Jesus will be the presence of God with his people. As 'the Alpha and the Omega, the First and the Last, the Beginning and the End' (v 13), Jesus is identifying with God (the Father);[3] in being their reward and repaying what the saints have done, he is fulfilling the role of God.[4] 'Anyone who has seen me has seen the Father.'[5] When Jesus returns, we will see God face to face.

There is another invitation, another longing – all who are thirsty should 'come' (v 17, TNIV). Without change and repentance, 'those who do wrong continue to do wrong' (v 11); when Jesus comes they will be shut off from the glory and wonder of the holy city. That is a double tragedy, since, though the offer of life came at great cost to Jesus and will involve costly faithfulness, it remains a free gift to all who will accept the invitation.

As you patiently await Jesus' coming, in what area of your life do you need to say again 'Come, Lord Jesus'?

[1] Rom 8:18 [2] Dan 8:26; 12:4 [3] See Rev 1:8; 21:6 [4] See Gen 15:1; Isa 40:10 [5] John 14:9

BIBLE IN A YEAR: **2 Kings 6,7; 2 Corinthians 4**

Ernest Lucas

HOW TO READ WISDOM LITERATURE

The wisdom literature comprises the books of Job, Proverbs, Ecclesiastes and a few psalms (Pss 1,34,37,49,73,111,112). These writings account for about two-thirds of the occurrences of the Hebrew words for 'wisdom', 'wise' and 'to be wise' in the Old Testament. There are other words that are characteristic of these books but uncommon elsewhere in the Old Testament, such as: understanding, intelligent, insight, stupid, scoffer, fool.

To read this literature well requires us to understand the meaning of 'wisdom' in Hebrew. It covers a wide range of abilities, from Solomon's ability to rule well and his knowledge of plants and animals[1] to various practical skills.[2] Wisdom in the Old Testament is *the ability to cope well with the demands of life*, what is today called *life-skill*. That is why English Bible translations sometimes use 'skill' rather than 'wisdom'. In the wisdom literature, wisdom has an intellectual dimension, involving knowledge, understanding and insight – and, crucially, a spiritual one. It must be grounded in 'the fear of the LORD'.[3] It is a gift of God but is also to be acquired and developed by learning.[4] While Proverbs deals with everyday life, Job, Ecclesiastes and the wisdom psalms grapple with the big questions of life, such as its meaning, suffering and death.

Most of the wisdom literature is written as Hebrew poetry. Knowing the basics of how this poetry works helps when reading: it depends primarily on *patterns of meaning* rather than sound (such as rhyme). The basic unit is a two-part sentence, and there are broadly three classes of these units, depending on the way the two parts relate to each other.

1 *Antithetic parallelism.* Here, the second half expresses a contrast to the first: 'Lazy hands make for poverty, but diligent hands bring wealth.'[5]

2 *Synonymous parallelism.* The second half repeats the essential point of the first, but in different words: 'Pride goes before destruction, a haughty spirit before a fall.'[6]

[1] 1 Kings 4:29–34 [2] Exod 31:6; Ezek 27:8,9 [3] Prov 9:10 [4] Prov 1:2–6 [5] Prov 10:4 [6] Prov 16:18

3 *Progressive parallelism*. The second half develops what has been said in the first in some way: 'Fools find no pleasure in understanding but delight in airing their own opinions.'[7]

There may also be figures of speech, such as 'Like apples of gold in settings of silver is a ruling rightly given'.[8]

When reading Hebrew poetry, one must not over-interpret it. The poet had a limited choice of words to use to express a contrast or similarity and so one should major on the main point made, not minor differences of meaning in the words chosen. When a figure of speech is used, the important thing is the main point of comparison, not the details of the imagery used.

Proverbs 10–31 contains sayings expressed in brief poetic sentences. A Hebrew proverb is not a law. It is a reflection on life, crystallised in a brief, memorable sentence. It *describes the norm*. It does not *express the inevitable*. While it is generally true that 'A gentle answer turns away wrath, but a harsh word stirs up anger',[9] experience teaches us that neither half of the sentence is inevitably the case. Life and humans are too complex for a brief sentence to sum up all the truth about a given situation! Part of wisdom is being aware of this and being able to assess when a proverb is appropriate.

Proverbs arise as reflections based on observations of life. The reader needs wisdom to know when to use a particular proverb. Sometimes it is appropriate to say, 'Do not answer fools according to their folly, or you yourself will be just like them'; but at other times 'Answer fools according to their folly, or they will be wise in their own eyes' is more relevant.[10] Many proverbs are simply observations. Therefore, it is important to compare one proverb with another to get a rounded view of what the wisdom teachers were saying. For example, on its own, 'A bribe is seen as a charm by the ones who give it; they think success will come at every turn'[11] might seem to encourage using bribes, but not when balanced with other verses.[12] The brevity of proverbs means that they often give a very black-and-white picture. This must be balanced by remembering that they express *norms* not *laws*. 'Those who trust in their riches will fall, but the righteous will thrive like a green leaf'[13] expresses what often happens, not what always does happen, as some of the laments in Psalms make clear.

[7] Prov 18:2 [8] Prov 25:11 [9] Prov 15:1 [10] Prov 26:4,5, TNIV [11] Prov 17:8 [12] Prov 15:27; 17:23 [13] Prov 11:28

Ernest Lucas

Proverbs 1–9 contains ten 'lessons' given by a father to his son, interspersed by speeches by Wisdom (who is personified as a woman) and other pieces. Some readers find the male-orientation of these chapters difficult, even offensively sexist. However, two points are important here. First, the use of gender-neutral language in many modern English translations hides the fact that as well as warning his son against dangerous women he warns him against sinful/wicked *men* (often translated as 'people') who might lead him astray. Also, these chapters balance 'dangerous women' by the figure of Woman Wisdom. Second, the Bible always comes to us from a specific cultural situation. Sometimes this is very different from ours. When reading it we have to try to understand what it is saying in its original context and then, to apply it appropriately, we must transpose its meaning into our context. This applies to difference in gender. Thus, female readers can transpose the honey-lipped woman of the father's warnings into a sweet-talking man on the prowl for a one-night stand.

The well-known story of Job is told in two prose narratives, which form the introduction and conclusion to a series of long poetic speeches by Job, his friends, Elihu and God. The book contains some guidelines for reading it. The first is that Job does not experience great suffering because he is a sinner, indeed he 'fears God and shuns evil'.[14] The second is that God is angry with Job's friends because they 'have not spoken the truth about me, as my servant Job has'.[15] Each of the friends holds rigidly to the view that Job's suffering shows that he is a great sinner. This leads them to present a false picture of God. Their speeches are examples of wrong theologies. However, although Job has spoken more truly about God than his friends did, his theology has its own errors. In his, justifiable, defence of his innocence he rightly complains to God, but because he shares his friends' view that only sinners should suffer, he goes too far. He charges God with being hostile towards him and seeking to destroy him.[16] He even charges God with bullying humans and with injustice in heedlessly destroying both the innocent and the wicked.[17] A third guideline in the book alerts us to the errors in Job's theology; his own, final confession.[18] Here he is not going back on his assertion of his innocence. He is admitting that his previous understanding of God was deficient and distorted. This brings about the fourth guideline, God's probing questions to Job.[19] They expose his lack

---

[14] Job 1:8 [15] Job 42:7, TNIV [16] Job 16:6–14 [17] Job 9:2–24 [18] Job 42:1–6 [19] Job 38–41

of knowledge and understanding of God and also that his view of God's purposes is too limited because it is very human-centred. The book of Job does not provide a neat and tidy answer to the problem of suffering but, read rightly, it provides deep insights which have enabled countless readers down the ages to cope with life when going through times of suffering.

Ecclesiastes contains the teaching of someone whom the compiler of the book calls 'Qoheleth' (Teacher/Preacher). Qoheleth searches for meaning in life. He tries to find it in pleasure, wealth or work, but without success. The sufferings and injustices of life and, above all, death, make finding meaning very difficult. His cry that 'All is *hebel*'[20] can be understood in various ways: absurd, enigmatic, meaningless, transient, vain. There is much debate about the many seemingly contradictory statements in the book.[21] They may arise from the way Qoheleth thinks. He sees reality as complicated. He cannot accept simplistic answers which either emphasise only one side of things or propose some compromising middle way. The apparent contradictions of life have to be accepted and faced, because the whole truth lies beyond the comprehension of the human mind. In all his perplexity, he maintains belief in a sovereign God, though one whose purposes are beyond his understanding.

A guide to reading the book is provided by 12:9–14. Here, the compiler commends the honesty and integrity of Qoholeth's provocative questionings but warns against pressing them too far. They should be pursued within the context of fearing God and keeping his commands.[22] In particular, he asserts that God will judge everyone, though he does not say when or how. The compiler is saying that Qoheleth's teaching is helpful but incomplete. Qoheleth repeatedly says that he has searched 'under the sun'[23] to find meaning. His thoughts are limited to this life alone, because he has no clear hope of life beyond death. The book shows us that there is room for honest questioning and doubt, but we need that wider view to cope with some of the complexities of life.

FOR FURTHER READING

Ernest Lucas, *Exploring the Old Testament, Vol. 3: The Psalms and Wisdom Literature*, SPCK and IVP, 2003

---

[20] See eg Eccl 1:2 [21] Eg Eccl 4:2,3; 9:4,5 [22] Echoes of Deut 6:1–6 [23] Eg Eccl 1:14

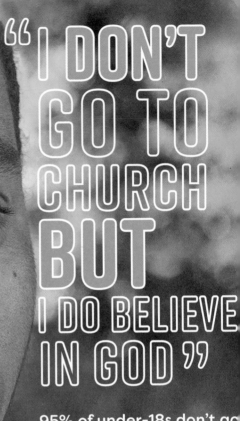

"I DON'T GO TO CHURCH BUT I DO BELIEVE IN GOD"

95% of under-18s don't go to church BUT many are open to exploring faith.

Together, we can reach the 95!
Find out more at **the95.org.uk**

Scriptu
Union

CONFLICTS AND RESOLUTIONS

The apostle Paul's relationship with the church in Corinth was not easy. He, with Aquila and Priscilla, had founded the church over eighteen months in AD 51 and 52, before departing for Ephesus, but he kept up a pastoral correspondence. He refers to an earlier letter that is now lost.[2] The Corinthians wrote back; their letter is also lost.[3] A variety of issues then arose to do with the health and good order of that gifted and growing congregation. Paul addressed them effectively in 1 Corinthians, but further complicating factors refused to make life easy, leading Paul to make a brief, extremely painful visit (2:1) and then to write a further letter 'with many tears' (2:4; 7:8) which is also lost. 2 Corinthians is the letter written by Paul in AD 57 after learning through Titus that the tearful letter, though it had caused hurt, had also achieved a result (7:6,7). By this Paul was deeply comforted, so much so that later he was able to return to Corinth and its local port Cenchreae, where he dispatched his famous letter to the Romans.[4]

If this seems complicated, it is nothing compared to the tangles in relationships that the letters reflect! But then, human beings have shown themselves well able to excel in misunderstandings and misrepresentation. Nor is this profound defect easily overcome within the churches, as experience makes clear. What is distinctive in this letter is the extent to which Paul reveals, and we glimpse, the heartfelt and physical sufferings that he underwent for the sake of Christ. Into no other apostle do we have such insights nor, we should add, do we encounter such personal confessions in much ancient literature. Once more, Paul shows himself to be extraordinary and, to be true to the man, he gives all the glory to God and takes none for himself (4:7).

Paul's conversion is a remarkable testimony to the truth of the risen Christ. So is his ability to endure.

Nigel G Wright

Acts 18:1–22 [2] 1 Cor 5:9 [3] 1 Cor 7:1 [4] Rom 16:1; compare the Gaius of Rom 16:23 with 1 Cor 1:14

2 Corinthians 1:1–11

Cross and Resurrection

Pray for grace today to 'read, mark, learn and inwardly digest'[1] the Word of God.

The themes of cross and resurrection permeate the whole of the New Testament. As Christ was raised out of death by God's power, so we can trust that, whatever befalls us in life, God can bring life from it (v 9). It requires a mighty leap of faith to believe this and the timescale is not for us to determine, but Christ defines who God is and what God can do and so the confidence has a solid foundation.

This is a comforting faith and it is no weakness to acknowledge that all of us need at times to be comforted. We might all share in the sufferings of Christ at some level. Paul could claim that he did so 'abundantly' (v 5) and he was not wrong. The precise nature of the troubles of which he speaks in verse 8 are not clear, but he has referred (probably metaphorically) to fighting with 'wild beasts in Ephesus'.[2] Paul was a brave man, but his was not a false machismo. He was emotional as well as passionate, vulnerable as well as resilient. He did not believe that as an apostle of Christ he was exempt from sufferings – quite the opposite: as a servant and apostle he was bound to suffer with Christ (v 5). He had looked into the abyss of death (v 9), but he was delivered and he trusted that God would again deliver him. Moreover, he saw in all of this a divine purpose: he was receiving God's comfort in Christ so that he might comfort others and they too might endure in the faith of Christ (v 6). This man's life was defined by God's overall purpose of salvation.

Let us admit it: in trouble and tragedy, in sorrow and sadness, we need the God who raises the dead. In him we place our trust.

'Taste and see that the LORD is good; blessed are those who take refuge in him.'[3]

[1] Thomas Cranmer, collect for the second Sunday in Advent [2] 1 Cor 15:32 [3] Ps 34:8, TNIV

BIBLE IN A YEAR: **2 Kings 8,9; Psalms 62,63**

2 Corinthians 1:12 – 2:4

The Wounded Healer

Give thanks today that you worship a God of infinite goodness.

We begin to catch glimpses of what has been going on. Accusations have been made against Paul's character. At some point he had stated his intention to make a prolonged visit to Corinth, visiting other churches on the way.[1] However, he had changed his plans after making his brief 'painful visit' (1:15,16; 2:1) – no doubt because he did not wish to cause further grief to the Corinthians and did not wish to be further distressed himself (v 3). Paul lived a highly stressful life. It is no surprise that he had a limit. As a consequence, there were those disposed against him who blackened his character by saying he was lacking in integrity and sincerity (1:12) and that he did not keep his word.

It is painful when people accuse us unjustly – but that is the way of the world (v 12). Humans are not so much guided by the will for truth as by the will for power: they seek advantage for themselves over others and what better way than by casting others in a bad light, implying false motives, spinning things in a negative direction? We see it all the time. Reluctantly, Paul defends himself and his fellow workers and insists that duplicity is not in their nature. If there was a change of plan there was wisdom in it. Their policy was to be true to Christ, in whom all God's promises are a straightforward 'Yes!' Is this our goal too?

It is striking in this letter how the sometimes unhappy dealings of the Corinthians become the occasion for profound statements of theology. Paul is operating on the level of deep theological reflection at the same time as dealing with our all-too-human failings. In Christ, God says 'Yes' to us (1:20). Christ is God's best and highest word.

Reflect on which of God's promises are 'Yes' in Christ. Which, in particular, do you most need to hear?

[1] 1 Cor 16:5–9

BIBLE IN A YEAR: **2 Kings 10–12; 2 Corinthians 5**

2 Corinthians 2:5–11

The Power of Forgiveness

Begin today by saying the Lord's Prayer.

In this letter we shall find even more derogatory accusations directed at Paul. As if all his apostolic sufferings were not enough, he has to cope with regular abuse from other believers. People have caused him grief (v 5) – and it hurts. By this time, he had come to expect opposition from outside the churches. From the time of his conversion, Jesus had warned him that this would come.[1] To be wounded by fellow believers, however, was a different matter and infinitely more painful.

This passage describes how the church in Corinth had disciplined one of its members. This is not the same case as that referred to in Paul's previous letter.[2] It relates rather to something that happened when Paul made his painful visit – indeed it may have been a major cause of the pain. Someone (a man) had verbally attacked Paul and publicly abused him. We speculate about his motives. The incident was damaging to Paul and the whole church (v 5). Now the church had taken the perpetrator in hand and made it clear that he had acted wrongly. This disapproval was probably all the punishment amounted to (v 6), but it was enough to provoke sorrow and bring redress. Now Paul urges forgiveness and the reaffirmation of love, adding that he too had let go of the offence and the offender, which is what forgiveness actually means (v 10). By letting go of animosity all round, no room is left for Satan, the accuser, to disrupt God's good work.

Sowing hostility through relationship breakdown is a satanic 'scheme' (see v 11). It inhibits the flow of love and trust and happens often, even where it should not. It is a device against which we should continually be on our guard. It is hurtful, an abomination to God. Repentance and forgiveness are the only remedy.

Pray: 'Search me, God, and know my heart … See if there is any offensive way in me.'[3]

[1] Acts 9:16 [2] 1 Cor 5:1–5 [3] Ps 139:23,24

BIBLE IN A YEAR: **2 Kings 13,14; 2 Corinthians 6**

Exultation!

Identify three things that bring you joy – and give thanks for them.

By now we may have the impression that Paul was capable of extremes of emotion. He moves from recalling the hurts of the past to exulting in the joy of the present. Exultation is the right word. What triggers this mood is meeting up with Titus, by whose hand he had sent his tearful letter. Paul leaves Ephesus for Troas (the ancient Troy) to preach – and also with the hope of meeting up with Titus to see whether reconciliation had been achieved. He is deeply anxious.

Troas was on the land route to Corinth (over 900 miles through Macedonia). They fail to connect, so Paul continues on and when he does finally locate Titus he receives the good news of the church's repentance.[1] Loving affection is restored. His relief and joy know no bounds. Once more, out of the grim details of his troubles Paul expresses his joy in sublime words.

To know Christ is to participate in a mighty victory. Paul likens it to the triumphal procession of a Roman general returning from foreign wars with booty and prisoners in his train. Christ is the victorious general (having triumphed over sin and death) and we are captives in his procession, yet willing captives. After anxiety and trouble, suddenly the mist clears and he sees that it is all worth it. All that has happened is part of a willing and grateful sacrifice that, as in the Old Testament, is a pleasing aroma rising to God.[2] The sacrifice is no longer that of bulls and goats but of those whose lives are being saved even while others may despise and oppose them (v 16). Through all his troubles, Paul can take pleasure that his conscience and ministry are clear (v 17).

Most of the time most of us live quite ordinary lives, but perhaps we, too, are given moments of exultation when everything seems worthwhile. Can you recall any? Give thanks.

[1] 2 Cor 7:5–7 [2] Eg Lev 1; Ps 141:2

BIBLE IN A YEAR: **2 Kings 15,16; Psalms 64,65**

2 Corinthians 3:1–6

Qualifications

God the Father 'has qualified you to share in the inheritance of his holy people in the kingdom of light'.[1]

Qualifications are important. Many have acquired bits of paper that certify they have demonstrated certain levels of knowledge or ability and therefore can be relied upon. There are, equally, many people who have achieved their qualifications in the university of life and probably believe them to be superior!

Paul, among the other things he had to endure, was subject to profound impertinence. He was the founder of the Corinthian church and had every right to believe that 'in Christ Jesus I became your father through the gospel'.[2] Now he is being asked by somebody (we shall come back to the question of who) to provide letters of recommendation to prove his bona fides (v 1). Should we put up with cheek, or should we name it for what it is? Paul gives the best possible answer, mixed up, again, with some decent theology: the Corinthians themselves were his recommendation. Through his ministry, Christ had become written on their hearts by the Spirit of the living God (note the trinitarian reference).

All this said, Paul introduces here the note of self-deprecation: he has no intention of commending himself since the facts speak for themselves. Anyway, what matters is not what we claim about ourselves but how we stand before God (v 4). If we have the power to accomplish anything for God it is because God has made it so. By grace, God has made him and his co-workers ministers of a new covenant, demonstrably so, one which operates in the life-giving Spirit (v 6). None of this means that qualifications don't matter – remember that Paul was a highly trained rabbinic scholar (as well as a tent-maker) and had worked hard to acquire the skills.[3] Without God's Spirit, however, this is all letters and not life.

Reflect prayerfully upon your qualifications, gifts and achievements. Give thanks for what God has given you and offer it back to be filled with the Spirit.

---

[1] Col 1:12 [2] 1 Cor 4:15 [3] Phil 3:4–6

BIBLE IN A YEAR: **2 Kings 17,18; 2 Corinthians 7**

2 Corinthians 3:7–18

Continuity and Contrast

On this Pentecost Sunday, continue to offer yourself up to the Spirit of God. Pray, 'Come, Holy Spirit!'

Mention of 'ministers of a new covenant' (v 6) sets Paul off in a wonderful direction. Understanding the relationship between Old and New Testaments (or covenants) is crucial if we are to read the Bible aright. The New grows out of the Old and is unintelligible without it. It does not merely repeat it but takes it to a new level, that is 'much more glorious' (v 9). There is therefore both continuity and contrast in the way Christians read the Hebrew scriptures. The new covenant both renews the story of redemption that has begun in the history of Israel and introduces new and crucial elements. These are focused in the revelation that comes in Christ (vs 12–16) and in the gift and coming of God's Spirit, through whom Christ's presence and work continue in the world (vs 17,18).

It is clear that Paul finds limitations in the old covenant given through Moses. Glorious though it was, it brings condemnation (v 9). It exposes the extent of human sin without providing the inner transformation needed to overcome it. The glory that was seen on Moses' face after his encounter with the Lord on Mount Sinai was radiant and powerful, so much so that Moses had to wear a veil.[1] This glory faded, however, and Jewish believers themselves have a veil when reading the scriptures and so do not see where it leads. Only in Christ is this taken away (v 14). By contrast, in the new covenant the glory of Christ never fades. Gazing upon him as we do, we undergo a steady transformation into his image (vs 16–18).

This is an apt reading for Pentecost. Worship is about turning to the Father through Christ in the Spirit and being changed as we do so. Keep coming back till the work is done.

'Turn your eyes upon Jesus; look full in his wonderful face.'[2]

[1] Exod 34:29–35 [2] Helen H Lemmel, 1922

BIBLE IN A YEAR: **2 Kings 19,20; 2 Corinthians 8**

2 Corinthians 4:1–6

The Face of Christ

'... the LORD make his face shine on you and be gracious to you.'[1]

We know what happened to Paul on the road to Damascus – a mighty conversion in which 'a light from heaven flashed around him'.[2] The rest truly is history. Paul encountered the risen Lord powerfully. Blinded as he was, we do not know whether he saw the Lord's face. Yet he could well have had this experience in mind when he recounted how God's light has shone into the hearts of believers, enabling us to see the glory of God in the face of Christ (v 6). There is a direct line from the God of creation to Christ as the revelation of God's glory: God revealing God's own self through God's own Son.

There are 42 individual muscles in the human face, enabling a hugely meaningful range of emotions to be expressed. This is not true of any other creature. We can only imagine the face of Christ, but we can be absolutely sure that it expresses the fullness of God's love, God's glory, God's beauty and God's holiness towards us. It suffuses us with light and banishes the darkness. In turn, this requires of those whom God calls that they renounce any forms of duplicity or distortion or shameful ways, most especially for those who are to be representatives of the ways of God, as Paul was (v 1). There is evidence enough that Paul feels impelled to say this because of accusations slurring his character and his ministry. Even so, he is not going to give up.

Whatever our calling, transparency is always the best policy. As God's light shines through the risen Lord, so his light should shine through us, that people might catch a glimpse of the King. Jesus daringly told his disciples, 'You are the light of the world.'[3] We are agents of the one who is the very Light of the world.[4]

Reflect: The church can never be the light of the world until Christ is the Light of the church.

[1] Num 6:25 [2] Acts 9:3 [3] Matt 5:14 [4] John 8:12

BIBLE IN A YEAR: **2 Kings 21,22; 2 Corinthians 9**

2 Corinthians 4:7–12

Treasure in Clay Pots

Pray, 'My sacrifice, O God, is a broken spirit; a broken and contrite heart you, God, will not despise.'[1]

It is a human disposition to boast. Apparently this was even more so in the classical world, as numerous ancient tablets and monuments testify. We see the same today in the art of the CV, in which applicants for jobs big themselves up and compete for attention. Having read a few, it surprises me that people aren't more ashamed than they are to boast of their alleged skills and achievements.

Clay pots are the delight of archaeologists because they are so common, found at any dig. Sometimes they actually contain valuables like hoards of silver coins. We see here how self-effacing Paul is. He is a clay pot: what is important is what it contains of God (v 7). Paul did not regard himself as a Christian celebrity, full of glamour and flashing teeth. Quite the opposite. He is forever 'being given over to death for Jesus' sake' (v 11). He boasts of his weakness and fragility, 'hard pressed on every side' (v 8) and yet, deep down, sustained by a resilience and ability to endure – strengths that can only be attributed to God.

Those who are unable to see the glory of Christ that is found in the light of the gospel (v 4) might have reason to make much of themselves, but those who have seen the face of Jesus Christ have something better to live for. Along with John the Baptist, they say, 'He must become greater; I must become less.'[2] There is a quite legitimate self-care by which we maintain the health of body, soul and spirit. Paul's pressures and problems were inflicted upon him by others rather than by himself (though no doubt he could have done better). It is not without cost, however, that we follow Christ – and neither should it be. Yet cross leads to resurrection; death to life (v 10).

Reflect: What did Jesus mean by saying, 'In this world you will have trouble'?[3]

[1] Ps 51:17 [2] John 3:30 [3] John 16:33

BIBLE IN A YEAR: **2 Kings 23–25; Psalms 66,67**

2 Corinthians 4:13–18

The Endurance of Faith

'I have fought the good fight, I have finished the race, I have kept the faith.'[1]

This passage begins and ends with faith. Faith is the ability to trust in that which we cannot see or touch, but which we are confident is both true and real (v 18). Faith is not therefore, as some claim, an illusory trust in that for which we have no evidence. Rather, the evidence is that God has raised Jesus from the dead (v 14) and is therefore able to do the impossible, to bring life from death.

When we consider all the troubles Paul had to endure (and we are not yet through), it is amazing to us that he did not just give up. Reliable tradition tells us that he would finally crown it all as a martyr in Rome in about AD 64. Yet he could have avoided all that suffering by opting for an easy life, perhaps by continuing to make his living as a prosperous tent-maker. Most of us have our limits, but apparently not Paul. He endured, and in this passage we see why and how.

It helped that he was seeing progress in his work. More and more people (v 15) were being reached by God's grace. In Troas he had found an open door for the gospel[2] – only his anxiety about Titus and Corinth led him to leave. More converts meant more thanksgiving and glory for God. His sufferings were not in vain. Most of all, however, he was inspired because he could see a future reality, unseen in the present but prefigured in the resurrection, a vision of future glory that would abundantly outweigh all present troubles. By contrast, all these were light and momentary (v 17). Imagining this glorious God-given future can inwardly renew us (v 16) and constantly impassion us. It is not beginning the race only but completing it that really matters.

'And let us run with perseverance the race marked out for us, fixing our eyes on Jesus, the pioneer and perfecter of faith.'[3]

---

[1] 2 Tim 4:7 [2] 2 Cor 2:12 [3] Heb 12:1,2

BIBLE IN A YEAR: 1 Chronicles 1–3; 2 Corinthians 10

Future Hope

The vision: 'He will wipe every tear from their eyes. There will be no more death ... the old order of things has passed away.'[1]

Christians disagree about the nature of the life to come. Some think we sleep in Christ until the day of resurrection and final judgement (v 10). Others imagine that, having died, we pass immediately and consciously into heaven. Others think that if we are sleeping anyway the first amounts to the second, to all intents and purposes. Yet others say that all we need to know is that when we are absent from the body we are with the Lord (v 8). In the meantime, we have the Spirit as the guarantee of greater life to come and while we are in the body we should get on with pleasing the Lord (v 9).

It is clear that Paul's train of thought on faith in the unseen leads him to dwell for some moments on high theological themes. We see this move from present troubles to deep theological truth frequently in this letter. It matters to Paul that we should have a body in which to dwell – otherwise we are 'naked' (v 3). Our present bodies are like an earthly tent, fragile and vulnerable and certainly mortal, subject to death and dying. Yet they are necessary: otherwise (literally) where would we be? In the future life, however, all this will be 'swallowed up by life' (v 4). So Paul seems not to fear the prospect of death but to look beyond it to a new world of resurrection existence that is imperishable, 'an eternal house in heaven' (v 1). Final judgement is not something to fear, but a resolution of everything that falls short in this life.

Being mortal, it is difficult for us not to shrink back from death; but here is a glorious hope that it is not the end but the beginning of life. There is love at the end.

Jesus said, 'I will come back and take you to be with me that you also may be where I am.'[2]

[1] Rev 21:4 [2] John 14:3

BIBLE IN A YEAR: 1 Chronicles 4–6; 2 Corinthians 11

2 Corinthians 5:11 – 6:2

Redemptive Solidarity

Prepare for today by reflecting on, 'For as in Adam all die, so in Christ all will be made alive'.[1]

Occasionally preachers talk about the Bible's 'purple passages'. They mean passages rich in theology and insight, full of meaningful truths, shaping and clarifying what we believe and how we live. This is one such, about how God has reconciled the world to God's own self, has done so through the work of Christ and now calls us to share in this work of restoring people and our world to God.

None of this could be said, of course, were it not true that God is a God who wills to save the world that he loves and has taken the initiative to do so. This is seen in the whole career of Jesus, in whom God has been present to redeem (v 19). We can call this 'redemptive solidarity', in that first of all God in Christ assumes our humanity so that Christ may do what we cannot do: he lives a life without sin,

one utterly pleasing to God, and then takes the sin of the world upon his own self as though he were a sinner. In doing so he effects a great exchange – he takes our sin, crucifies it and buries it in the tomb and we receive his righteousness in return (v 21). Because as God's gift he died for all of us, we have all died (vs 14,15). When here it says 'all' surely it means what it says: everybody.

Such belief changes the way we look at the world. We see it through different eyes. We view people as those who can, in Christ, become new creatures (v 17). We see ourselves as now under an obligation of thanksgiving, to live for Christ, not just for ourselves (v 15) and to become ambassadors of reconciliation for him (v 20). This was Paul's task. It is also ours.

Reflect: What does it mean to be an 'ambassador'? Whom do ambassadors represent? How should they speak and what should they speak about?

---

[1] 1 Cor 15:22

BIBLE IN A YEAR: 1 Chronicles 7–10; Psalm 68

2 Corinthians 6:3–13

Living Free

'Let me be full, let me be empty, let me have all things, let me have nothing.'[1]

Paul's hardships and the need to renew affection with the Corinthian church are never far away. Talk of reconciliation means that he must return to the task of setting things right. Reconciliation requires work from both ends: Paul has opened his heart wide and appeals to his 'children' to do the same (vs 11–13).

Given all that Paul endures for the gospel, some of it listed here, we continue to be amazed that he is so resilient. He rises above all he suffers and he keeps bouncing back. In order not to put stumbling blocks in anybody's pathway to Christ and in Christ, he has trained himself to rise above all his afflictions and to find in Christ and his gospel a centre and resource that sustain him. In Christ and by the Spirit (v 6) he can take it all and yet still find a way to rejoice and to feel himself rich, 'having nothing, and yet possessing everything' (v 10). There is something deeply Christian in this. We can clearly see all the afflictions of these verses in the life and death of Jesus: neither Paul nor we are above our Lord. Beyond that still, we can trace the love of God who, in Christ, was reconciling the world to himself.

Do we also find here an unhealthy martyr-complex, a troubling delight in suffering? Some may find Paul at fault here. Others would find in it a kind of 'purity' (v 6). We might both admire Paul's fortitude and yet also issue a warning: if we are called to follow a similar path we must be sure it is for Christ's sake, not to satisfy something within ourselves. That would still be a form of self-centredness, falling short of 'For to me, to live is Christ'.[2]

'A Christian is the most free lord of all, and subject to none; a Christian is the most dutiful servant of all, and subject to every one.'[3]

---

[1] From *The Methodist Covenant Prayer* [2] Phil 1:21 [3] Martin Luther, *On the Freedom of a Christian*, 1520

BIBLE IN A YEAR: **1 Chronicles 11–14; 2 Corinthians 12**

The Ultimate Statistic

Confess your faith: 'The LORD is my shepherd, I lack nothing.'[1]

This psalm is unusual in that it is not addressed to God but to people, in fact to all people (v 1). It seems to have more in common with Proverbs or Ecclesiastes than with Israel's hymn book. While people might jibe that 'religion' is about 'pie in the sky when you die', the Old Testament refutes that claim. It is widely recognised that it contains no developed doctrine of a life to come. Death is the common end for both man and beast (v 14), though perhaps the 'shades' of the dead continue in a shadowy and unattractive 'realm of the dead' (Hebrew: *Sheol*), never to see the light of life again (vs 11,15,19). The point is that this is everybody's fate, high and low, wealthy, wise, foolish and senseless. Whatever the boasts and splendour of the fortunate, it is all destined to end in the same way – decay and dust (v 14). Moreover, there is no way out. Nobody can redeem us from our common fate (v 7). Israel hoped for pie in this life, not beyond it.[2]

However, we may pick up the themes of continuity and contrast between the Testaments. There is continuity in that life ends in death for all of us, but there is a pivotal event that changes everything: 'we are convinced that one died for all, and therefore all died … if anyone is in Christ, the new creation has come.'[3] There is, after all, a Redeemer who can ransom us for God, despite verse 7! There is something radically 'new' in the new covenant: abundant life in the now *and* in the life to come. Death is no longer our shepherd (v 14). We have another.[4]

Perhaps there is just a hint of this in verse 15: God 'will surely take me to himself'. A well-placed hope.

'I have come that they may have life, and have it to the full.'[5]

[1] Ps 23:1 [2] Though notice how the hope for resurrection begins in Dan 12:1–4 [3] 2 Cor 5:14,17 [4] John 10:14 [5] John 10:10

BIBLE IN A YEAR: **1 Chronicles 15,16; 2 Corinthians 13**

In Step with God

'Although the whole world is mine, you will be for me a kingdom of priests and a holy nation.'[1]

When we compare 6:13 with 7:2, the intervening parts of today's passage appear to interrupt Paul's appeal for reconciliation. It is widely thought, therefore, that this is an inserted fragment of another letter, possibly from an earlier one Paul wrote, now lost.[2] This is plausible (although only a theory), in that the theme has to do with separation and Paul thinks he may have been misunderstood.

Certainly these verses are about separating from evil practices and persons. The emphasis is binary: there is nothing in common between righteousness and wickedness, light and darkness, Christ and Belial (a word for 'worthlessness', possibly meaning the devil), the Temple of God and idols (vs 14–16). The logic and the outcome are clear: Don't go there! We are called to be holy, to keep in step with God and to be God's alone (v 16). In certain areas there can be no compromise between good and evil. 'Cut it out' is the appropriate response. This can be misunderstood, however. Although some Christians are too quick to compromise, their example has led others to go too far the other way, to drastic forms of separation and the refusal to participate in aspects of social life that are in themselves wholesome or morally neutral, activities where Christians might be salt and light.[3] This may be the significance of 1 Corinthians 5:9–13, where Paul clarifies what he did or did not mean by his advice. Withdrawal from society was not on his agenda.

For most of us this is not the problem. Rather, we might succumb to the subtle pressures that society and commerce impose upon us. 'Purity' (see 6:6) is not a popular word in our world, seen as old-fashioned, to say the least. Perhaps it is time to reinstate it.

'Create in me a pure heart, O God, and renew a steadfast spirit within me ... I will teach ... so that sinners will turn back to you.'[4]

---

[1] Exod 19:5,6 [2] 1 Cor 5:9 [3] Matt 5:13–16 [4] Ps 51:10,13

BIBLE IN A YEAR: 1 Chronicles 17,18; Galatians 1

2 Corinthians 7:3–16

The Wounds of a Friend

'If it is possible, as far as it depends on you, live at peace with everyone.'[1]

Now Paul is back on track, reconciling fully with the Corinthians. We have more details of his anxiety on account of the rupture and of his profound relief once he had met Titus and learnt that his hurtful letter (v 8) had yielded dividends (vs 6,7). It is interesting that sometimes when there has been a falling out and then a reconciliation the renewed relationship can be on a deeper level. There is evidence of that here. Sadly it is not always the case.

There is still some business to clear up. Paul regretted having hurt his friends, but at the same time he didn't (vs 8–10). We don't like to hurt people, or to be hurt by them, but sometimes difficult things have to be done and said, even if it would be easier not to. Paul comes up with a new term here: 'godly sorrow' (see v 10). There is a difference between remorse and repentance. We might regret doing a wrong thing because we were found out and don't like the consequences – but we would do it again if we could get away with it. Or we might genuinely feel that we fell short of being our best selves, we failed God and each other, and set ourselves to change. This is godly sorrow because it wants 'to see justice done' (v 11), to resolve things. How much better we feel when we have done so!

When relationships are tangled, sometimes we need someone to help us, to go where we cannot, to act as a mediator. Tribute should be paid here to Titus, Paul's co-worker (vs 13–16). Paul will not boast of himself, but he does so of Titus, an agent of reconciliation, a peacemaker, who came to be loved equally by both parties to the dispute. Truly a servant of God.

Reflect: do you need to make peace with someone? 'Blessed are the peacemakers, for they will be called children of God.'[2]

---

[1] Rom 12:18 [2] Matt 5:9

BIBLE IN A YEAR: 1 Chronicles 19–21; Psalm 69

The Relief Fund

Reflect today on what you are doing with your time, your talents and your money.

There are abrupt changes of direction in this letter. This has led some to speculate that it is not one letter but a compendium of several. Alternatively, we might imagine that, having met up with Titus, Paul is now dictating the letter during his long journey (the distance by road from Ephesus to Corinth via Troas is over 900 miles). He has a mental list of items to address and having reconciled with the church he is now able to deal with them. This section deals with Paul's grand project, the world's first international rescue fund, destined for the church in Jerusalem. Equality and generosity are his themes.

Interestingly, Paul never mentions money (perhaps it embarrassed him). Instead, he goes for the heart. For him, the example of Jesus is what determines everything. In a further flight of fine theology, he speaks of Christ who was rich, yet for our sakes became poor (v 9). Out of grace, Christ exchanges his riches for our poverty, making us rich in spiritual grace. He is the supreme example of what it means to give, so imaging the love of God. This is where the inspiration to give comes from, as the Macedonian churches Paul has passed through on the way have already demonstrated (vs 1,2). Accordingly, giving can be invited but not commanded (v 5). It should spring from a willing heart (vs 11,12) and should be proportionate (v 12) though also sacrificial (v 2). And it should aim at equality (vs 13,14).

Equality is a slippery concept. We are all equal in God's eyes – and yet by any worldly standards there is great inequality. Some have and some have not, so it is just and right that those who have should show care for those who have not. The implications of such a principle are massive. We should work them out.

'Give, and it will be given to you ... For with the measure you use, it will be measured to you.'[1]

[1] Luke 6:38

BIBLE IN A YEAR: **1 Chronicles 22,23; Galatians 2**

2 Corinthians 8:16 – 9:5

Doing the Right Thing

'Give, and it will be given to you. A good measure, pressed down, shaken together and running over.'[1]

We could gain the impression that Paul travelled alone, but this was rarely so.[2] In addition to Timothy,[3] we have met Titus and now we have reference to two unnamed but acclaimed 'brothers' (vs 18,22) whom Paul is sending on ahead with Titus to manage the collection for the saints in Jerusalem. The apostolic mission is a collective effort, carried through by gifted, enthusiastic (v 17) and zealous (v 22) servants of God. There are still such 'representatives of the churches' (v 23) today, for whom we give thanks. We always need more. It is clear that Paul is deflecting any possible suspicion about how the fund will be used (v 20). Quite right. If it seems risky to carry a large sum of money all the way to Jerusalem, as it must have been, we do have precedent. Every year, Jews of the dispersion were charged a Temple tax that had to be delivered in like manner. Paul's fund, however, is a gift, not a tax.

Financial propriety is a Christian discipline. Paul terms it 'to do what is right' in God's eyes as well as those of other people (v 21). The principle could be extended to other legitimate areas of accountability, not only to the community but to the governing authorities. We return to the idea of transparency. The overall concern is to maintain the integrity of the churches and so to bring honour to Christ.

The topic of money is often a prickly one to deal with. These chapters show us some principles to guide us in our personal stewardship and pose a challenge. The more we give, the more we may make others rich. The more we have, the more opportunity we have to do good. 'It is more blessed to give than to receive.'[4]

It is said that John Wesley taught, 'Earn all you can, give all you can, save all you can.' What do you make of this principle?

---

[1] Luke 6:38 [2] Eg Acts 20:4 [3] 2 Cor 1:1 [4] Acts 20:35

BIBLE IN A YEAR: **1 Chronicles 24–27; Galatians 3**

Health and Wealth

Take stock today of the ways in which you have been blessed. Do not take any of it for granted. Give thanks to God for everything.

We hear from some quarters about the so-called 'health and wealth' gospel – the idea that if we trust in God then good health and overflowing wealth are as good as guaranteed. For some it is an enticing doctrine, yet it seems to bear no relation to the 'man of sorrows, and acquainted with grief'[1] we recognise in Jesus, nor indeed to Paul's own sufferings. Then again, it is not as though God wants us to be sick and to live in poverty! This passage has much to say about the generosity of God towards us and God's ability 'to bless you abundantly, so that … you will abound in every good work' (v 8). There is indeed a promise here that those who freely take the risk of giving all to God and imitating God's generosity will have no cause to fear that they will go without (v 6).

What is at stake is the difference between a promise and a technique. Once we have turned faith into a technique by which we manipulate God, to gain a particular advantage, we have certainly gone astray. That is a pagan, not Christian, way of relating to God, an attempt to magic out of God what we believe to be in our own self-interest. This is not what Paul speaks of here. He is concerned with the God of promise who can be trusted to provide for those who freely trust him. God gives generously so that we may live generously (v 11). In view here are the poor (v 12), not already wealthy organisations or individuals.

It is true that we reap what we sow. What we give out determines what we receive back. Sowing is a specific and intentional action, a task that we deliberately set about. Let's always turn in that direction.

'To those who by persistence in doing good seek glory, honour and immortality, he will give eternal life.'[2]

---

[1] Isa 53:3, ESV [2] Rom 2:7

BIBLE IN A YEAR: 1 Chronicles 28,29; Psalms 70,71

Corinthians 10:1–6

True and False Ministry

Pray today, 'Lead me, LORD, in your righteousness because of my enemies – make your way straight before me.'[1]

Paul's letter makes another abrupt turn. On his list of 'matters to be dealt with' is a clash of interests with a group of what he calls 'super-apostles'.[2] After he had laid the foundations of the church,[3] other ministers had come on the scene. Apollos was a glamorous and eloquent preacher whose influence was beneficial.[4] However, his 'great fervour'[5] may just have overexcited the church, such that when a band of triumphalist, Jewish-heritage[6] super-apostles then appeared it was taken in by their big talk and subtly turned against Paul. Here is the source of some of the undermining comments Paul endured, including the demand for letters of reference[7] and the suggestion here that his presence was less impressive than his written warnings (v 1).

Paul is anticipating conflict with this group. Perhaps he is warning himself not to go over the top! He appeals first to the humility and gentleness of Christ and then renounces worldly methods. The weapons available to him in combating falsehood and 'strongholds' (v 4) that resist God are spiritual: prayer, faith, the statement of the truth, the Holy Spirit. Christ is the lens through which all arguments are to be viewed and brought into line (v 5). Every thought needs to be in harmony with him. Paul clearly prefers to come 'in love and with a gentle spirit' rather than with the rod of discipline,[8] but if he has to get tough he will do so (v 6).

Still it is not clear what 'getting tough' means. At most it would mean excluding troublemakers from the community. Christians do not pursue godly ends by ungodly means. What is evil, delusional or deceptive is not resisted by returning like for like: this is just recycling. Evil has to be overcome by its opposite.

'Be careful to do what is right in the eyes of everyone ... Do not be overcome by evil, but overcome evil with good.'[9]

[1] Ps 5:8 [2] 2 Cor 11:5 [3] 1 Cor 3:6 [4] Acts 18:24–28 [5] Acts 18:25 [6] 2 Cor 11:5,6 [7] 2 Cor 3:1–6 [8] 1 Cor 4:21 [9] Rom 12:17,21

BIBLE IN A YEAR: **2 Chronicles 1,2; Galatians 4**

Gratitude in Worship

'Thanks be to God for his indescribable gift!'[1]

This is another psalm addressed not to God but to Israel, ascribed to Asaph, a Temple worship-leader and songwriter described elsewhere as 'Asaph the seer'.[2] He had inspired gifts. We imagine this psalm being delivered prophetically during Temple services. It is an exhortation to sincerity of life and worship.

The first part addresses the faithful and portrays God surrounded by fire and tempest (v 3). This holy and disturbing God is judging the covenant people as their God, the God of righteousness and justice (v 6). God is not displeased with their sacrifices, but he takes pains to say that he does not need them. If God were hungry, which he is not, all the creatures of the field are already his. God does not need the flesh or blood. These are symbols only, not food for the deity. What satisfies God is heartfelt thanksgiving, loyalty and humble prayer (vs 12–15,23). What God hates is hypocrisy, ritual acts of religion that are not expressions of a good life but mask all manner of corrupt behaviour and backbiting (vs 16–21).

Christians do not have to offer animal sacrifices to God – churches would resemble shambles (butchers' shops)! Here too we encounter the themes of continuity and contrast. Animal sacrifices are no longer part of our devotion, but what they symbolise certainly is: the offering of our own lives in thanksgiving and service, offerings made personally and privately as well as when we gather. Made also through the sacraments and ordinances that focus us upon God's love in Christ. God looks upon the heart. Words and acts are not enough on their own: only when backed by dispositions and deeds.

'To worship is to quicken the conscience by the holiness of God, to feed the mind with the truth of God, to purge the imagination by the beauty of God, to open the heart to the love of God, to devote the will to the purpose of God.'[3]

[1] 2 Cor 9:15 [2] 2 Chr 29:30 [3] Archbishop William Temple, 1881–1944

BIBLE IN A YEAR: **2 Chronicles 3–5; Galatians 5**

2 Corinthians 10:7–18

Boasting in the Lord

'...but let those who boast boast about this: that they understand and know me, that I am the LORD, who exercises kindness.'[1]

We should always remember that every story has two sides. As regards all that was happening in Corinth we only have one side – Paul's. We entertain the possibility that Paul may be being a tad unfair. This said, we incline towards giving him the benefit of the doubt, not least because he was clearly the target of serious misrepresentation.

We learn more here about the accusation that in person Paul was unimpressive and ineffectual (v 10). He also stands accused of using threatening language (v 9). Perhaps it is even being claimed that he is not a proper Christian (v 7) and that he is sinfully boastful. He does indeed own up to a certain kind of boasting, but it is boasting in the Lord (v 17) of what God has achieved through him, not least in reaching Corinth with the gospel (v 14). In making it clear that he had a commission from the risen Lord and the authority that went with it (v 8), Paul could easily be accused of a form of self-aggrandisement – but he was also stating a fact. Paul is clear about his limits. He was not going to take the credit for what others had achieved (unlike his opponents) and was looking forward to boasting about new regions opening up beyond Corinth (vs 15,16). Good boasting!

Sadly, here in the early origins of the Christian church we find evidence of a competitive and factional spirit. We would like to report that this was swiftly and decisively overcome, but even the powerful words of Paul's hymn to love previously addressed to Corinth[2] could not avert it. For all that we go on reading Paul's letters, this factional spirit continues to this day. The remedy will not be found until the time comes when each of us resolves never to be part of it.

'Do nothing out of selfish ambition or vain conceit. Rather, in humility value others above yourselves.'[3]

---

[1] Jer 9:24, TNIV [2] 1 Cor 13 [3] Phil 2:3

BIBLE IN A YEAR: **2 Chronicles 6,7; Galatians 6**

Fighting the Good Fight

'He gave his life to purchase freedom for everyone. This is the message God gave to the world at just the right time.'[1]

It becomes clearer what is at stake. Paul is fighting to keep the Corinthians in the faith by rescuing them from versions of Jesus, the Spirit and the gospel that differ from those he introduced them to (vs 3,4). They are at risk of being deceived by Satan masquerading as an angel of light (vs 13–15). For Paul, no struggle could be more important.

There are more criticisms of Paul. This time the charge is ironic. Paul has been scrupulous in his financial probity to the point of refusing to accept financial help from the Corinthians. Instead, alongside working at his trade, he has relied upon the churches of Macedonia to fund his ministry in Corinth (vs 7–9). He is now being faulted for not taking money! Perhaps behind this there is some disdain for manual workers. Disdain is also evident in that he is being written off as a rhetorician (v 6). The super-apostles are classing Paul as inferior to themselves (v 5), setting him off along the 'foolish' path of proving the opposite (vs 1,12).

At stake is the matter of control. The super-apostles are wresting the church from Paul's influence because they want to control it (v 20). We infer that they themselves have no hesitation in accepting financial support and argue it is a privilege for the Corinthians to support them.[2] The question of control distinguishes a free Christian community from a cult. Crucially, Paul has never had ambitions to wed them to himself but only to Christ (v 2), whom to serve is perfect freedom. The Corinthians had previously made the mistake of thinking that when they were baptised by someone, they were bound to that person.[3] Not so. Christ alone is Lord and he does not delegate his lordship.[4]

'It is for freedom that Christ has set us free. Stand firm, then, and do not let yourselves be burdened again by a yoke of slavery.'[5]

[1] Tim 2:6, NLT [2] See also 2 Cor 2:17 [3] 1 Cor 1:12–17 [4] 1 Cor 12:3 [5] Gal 5:1

BIBLE IN A YEAR: **2 Chronicles 8,9; Psalm 72**

2 Corinthians 11:16–33

Foolish Talk

'I consider everything a loss because of the surpassing worth of knowing Christ Jesus my Lord, for whose sake I have lost all things.'[1]

This a remarkable passage, containing sarcasm directed at the Corinthians (vs 19,20) and irony directed at Paul's own self. He is driven to something he knows it is folly to do – boasting. In addition, he can distinguish between what he is doing and what Jesus would never do (v 17). He is riled! What follows is a CV like no other and, as far as the world is concerned, one not likely to land him a job. In short, Paul portrays himself as a loser for Christ's sake.

Consider this catalogue of rejection, torture, punishment and degradation. This makes sense of how Paul can say, 'I fill up in my flesh what is still lacking in regard to Christ's afflictions'[2] and 'We always carry around in our body the death of Jesus'.[3] How many are entitled to say this? Apparently, when the heroes of old boasted of their achievements, the greatest accolade to have received after storming a castle wall in battle, was the 'Corona Muralis', the equivalent of the Victoria Cross or the Medal of Honour.[4] Paul's travels, too, had included a wall, but he was heading in the wrong direction (vs 32,33)! This is self-deprecating boasting, but it adds to Paul's moral authority. We may struggle to fit all his sufferings into the narratives of the Acts of the Apostles. Either the author (assume Luke) did not know about them all or Paul wasn't telling, except here.

Paul is often caricatured as a stern, intolerant and unyielding puritan. He had his moments. Now, however, we can see him, probably more than any figure of the ancient world other than Jesus, as loving, passionate, generous, faithful, stupendously brave and utterly devoted to Christ. How much is there here to imitate, by grace? Was he a loser or a winner?[5]

Reflect: It is better to fail in an enterprise that will ultimately succeed than to succeed in an enterprise that will ultimately fail.

---

[1] Phil 3:8 [2] Col 1:24 [3] 2 Cor 4:10 [4] See Tom Wright, *Paul: A Biography*, SPCK, 2018, 314–315 [5] Phil 1:21

BIBLE IN A YEAR: **2 Chronicles 10–12; Ephesians 1**

2 Corinthians 12:1–10

Touching Heaven and Earth

Call to mind some of the peak experiences of God in your own life. What do you consider to be their importance now?

Having started boasting, Paul decides to finish the job. Although he refers obliquely to someone in the third person, he means himself and describes experiences he had in the Spirit. 'Fourteen years' previously (see v 2) would place these experiences in about 42–43 AD, prior to his first missionary journey. The 'third heaven' (v 2) is the very presence of God, where he heard inexpressible things (v 4). If a mystic is a person who is given intense spiritual experiences, then Paul, in addition to everything else, was a mystic. He is reluctant to speak of these experiences. Acts rarely refers to them, apart from his conversion.

For Paul, it is not mystic states that lend him credibility but words and deeds (v 6). There is no doubt that many who are Christians are so because of profound spiritual encounters with God. Probably the 'super-apostles'[1] were making their own supernatural claims, so this is a reminder that we should always be discerning. Credulity is not the same as faith. Faith is trusting in God's specific promises that are '"Yes" in Christ'[2] – not believing anything we are told. Satan is able to appear as an 'angel of light'.[3] Such proper caution, however, should not lead us to be disrespectful of people's spiritual experiences when they are accompanied by other indications of their genuineness.

Amidst it all, Paul is kept down to earth by what he calls a 'thorn in my flesh' (v 7), a weakness of some kind (nobody has worked out what) that seems to have been publicly known and requires him to depend upon God. He has learnt a great secret. Victory in Christ is not about us but about Christ being seen in us, even at our weakest.

Where do you particularly need to depend upon God for grace? Can you take a positive approach to this, in the wider purposes of God for your life?

[1] 2 Cor 11:5 [2] 2 Cor 1:20 [3] 2 Cor 11:14

BIBLE IN A YEAR: **2 Chronicles 13–15; Ephesians 2**

2 Corinthians 12:11–21

Reconciliation on the Way

'As I have loved you, so you must love one another. By this everyone will know that you are my disciples, if you love one another.'[1]

Paul now anticipates his third arrival in Corinth (v 14).[2] His first visit was when he established the church with 'signs, wonders and miracles' (v 12). The second was the painful visit that left him badly wounded. Now he is sending Titus and others ahead, bearing his completed letter, and anticipates with some anxiety a full reconciliation. Some pain, seemingly, remains (vs 13,16), but by the grace of God Paul believes himself more than equal to the super-apostles, if they are still around. Perhaps they have moved on somewhere else to flaunt their egos and burnish their credentials. They have also left the suspicion that Paul's intention was to exploit the church, a criticism he refutes by indicating how little he or Titus or their co-workers laid burdens on them (vs 16–18).

What Paul still fears is further grief and a badly diseased church (v 21), even though there is now reason to hope that the worst is past. The depth of his love for the Corinthians is evident (vs 14,15). In the event, all will be well: while in Corinth, Paul will find space and time to write his great letter to the Romans, before his final journey to Jerusalem.

Church is supposed to be a safe place where we do not hurt each other or cause one another to stumble. Most of the time it is but, as with families, it is sometimes those who mean most to us to whom we are most vulnerable. We owe it to each other to safeguard our churches, not only for children and the elderly but for all people. The table around which we meet for communion is a symbol of hospitality, generosity, gift and grace. This is what it rightly means to be church. When it succeeds there is great joy.

Can your church say: 'Come with us and we will treat you well, for the LORD has promised good things to Israel'?[3]

---

[1] John 13:34,35   [2] See also 2 Cor 13:1   [3] Num 10:29

BIBLE IN A YEAR: **2 Chronicles 16,17; Psalm 73**

Journey's End

At the end of this letter, identify what in particular has struck you and what you will take away from it.

Having been impressively tender, Paul now shows himself to be tough, still concerned that there might be a wilfully sinful minority disrupting the church (v 2).[1] He is prepared to face up to them, indeed he has authority from Christ to do so (v 10). He is reluctant to be harsh but will not shirk his duty. To hold to the truth in word and deed is his watchword (v 8), and a good one. To this end, he requires all to 'Examine yourselves to see whether you are in the faith; test yourselves' (v 5). This is a good thing to do every time we receive communion,[2] but not just then. Are we living in ways that are consistent with the faith we profess, with the Christ who is within us? Or are we deceiving ourselves?

It is entirely right that every church should be an inclusive community that welcomes people of all kinds to find life in Christ. Much depends on this, if we are to fulfil the purposes of God. But it is also right to ask what we are prepared to exclude. Whereas we welcome all manner of people we do not embrace all manner of behaviour.[3] There is a call to repentance and newness of life if we are to be of the truth. The weakness to which Paul refers in verse 4 is not moral weakness but suffering.

The full restoration that Paul hopes for is not only one where the breech with himself is overcome, but one in which the church community is marked by rejoicing, encouragement, unity of mind and peaceful friendships (v 11). This becomes a possibility for all of us when we participate truly in the grace, love and fellowship that are ours in the God who is Father, Son and Spirit.

'There is neither Jew nor Gentile, neither slave nor free, nor is there male and female, for you are all one in Christ Jesus.'[4]

See also 2 Cor 12:21 [2] 1 Cor 11:28 [3] 2 Cor 12:20,21 [4] Gal 3:28

BIBLE IN A YEAR: **2 Chronicles 18–20; Ephesians 3**

Psalm 51

Purging the Guilt

If you can remember it or find it, repeat slowly the words of the General Confession.[1]

This psalm is credibly identified as King David's response to the prophet Nathan's direct exposure of his sin. He had committed adultery with Bathsheba and, even worse, when she became pregnant he schemed to make sure that her husband Uriah, a brave and honourable soldier, was killed in battle.[2] By now David was a successful and admired king of Israel who had everything he could ever need. His actions were utterly selfish and cold-blooded. He hoped nobody would notice. The guilt exposed by Nathan was deep. After this, David's reign turned sour. The psalm uses the language of deep repentance. It is sufficiently general that any guilty person could use it: and we are all guilty.

Repentance involves facing the truth about ourselves and feeling the depth of the wrong we have done (v 3). This is not pathological but realistic. The apostle Paul calls it 'godly sorrow' because it leads to changes of behaviour.[3] If we never feel sorrow over our sin, this itself is a form of hard-heartedness or self-delusion of which we need to repent. Sometimes we need to be brought up with a jolt (as David was) to face the truth. Sometimes, however, we are so shaken that it seems that our whole lives, from our mother's womb (v 5), have been wretched and worthless. Sometimes the sense of guilt does not easily disappear but needs to be deeply purged before we gain release (v 7). We feel the stain of sin.

Release is possible. God is our Saviour, who stands ready to hear our confession and to respond to it, not with further recrimination but with mercy, compassion and cleansing (vs 1,2). Christians know this because God's own Son has 'made intercession for the transgressors'[4] and God's own Spirit can truly make us clean (v 10).

'But if anybody does sin, we have an advocate with the Father – Jesus Christ, the Righteous One.'[5]

---

[1] *Book of Common Prayer*, Cambridge University Press, 2004 [2] 2 Sam 11,12 [3] 2 Cor 7:10 [4] Isa 53:12; Luke 23:34 [5] 1 John 2:1

BIBLE IN A YEAR: **2 Chronicles 21–23; Ephesians 4**

Scripture Union

By purchasing *Encounter with God*, you are helping to support Scripture Union's mission with children and young people. Thank you!

Subscribe to our free supporter and prayer magazine at su.org.uk/ connectingyou

2 Samuel 1–9

EARTHLY KINGS AND HEAVENLY REALMS

These passages offer timeless, daily challenges, as we read how individual choices affect whole families, their legacies and their relationships: choices which lead to murder, betrayal, love, envy – it is all here. With cautionary hindsight, we witness mighty men rise and fall, we see human strength emboldened by God or totally quashed by him. We witness human self-seeking in preference to seeking God's heart and how those with great potential can rise and fall.

As disciples, we understand the complexity of daily choices, but that is compounded here by promises of power and untold wealth. We are challenged to keep focused on the eternal, to avoid turning our eyes to the immediate glitter. Every story has two sides and these are no exception – Saul, who reigned for so long, fades disappointingly in comparison to David, the shepherd boy. Through David, God saw fit to establish an earthly throne of enormous influence and power and to go beyond David's comprehension by declaring that this was the never-ending kingdom.

The messianic throne of David would become clearer as the ages passed, revealed through a king who would leave everlasting glory to be born in a lowly place, to be crowned with thorns and to die. While other kings came and went, God was establishing a new kingdom built on decades of faithful servants, many of whom struggled and seemed insignificant When they handed that insignificance to God and walked with him, when they obeyed God before their own desires, God revealed himself. We will read of changing kings and kingdoms, of divided houses being reunited, but what never has, or will, change is the overriding narrative throughout this story (and all stories): the King of Kings is the one who has been, who will be and who always is to come.

Andy Robinson

FOR FURTHER READING

David Tsumura, *NICOT The Second Book of Samuel*, Eerdmans, 2019

K. Chafin, *The Preacher's Commentary, 1 & 2 Samuel*, Thomas Nelson, 1989

R Alter, *The David Story: A Translation with Commentary of 1 and 2 Samuel*, WW Norton, 2000

The Lord's Anointed

Thank you, Lord, for your faithfulness, even when I have been unfaithful. Thank you that you'll never leave my side or drive me from you.

Who killed Saul? There are three accounts in Scripture.[1] Today's text has stirred debate surrounding the underlying reasoning for the actions of this Amalekite. He may have been a battle scavenger who had come across Saul and expected praise and reward from David, whom Saul was pursuing. Is it by chance that he brings David the very items he would require when anointed king? He then presents himself as a resident alien, thereby expecting privileges under the Mosaic law – privileges he did not deserve. He tragically failed to understand the man of God that David was, or that David himself had had the opportunity to kill Saul.

David knew that if God had called and anointed Saul, who was he to take that sovereignty away? By his own words, this man sealed his fate. For if he *had* killed Saul, he had killed the Lord's anointed.[2] If he had not, he was still an Amalekite and had to die.[3] David ordered his death. In doing so, he shows that he had no hand in Saul's death, as many may have suspected; instead he mourned Saul, mourning we can take as genuine for, whatever Saul's failings, he was the Lord's anointed.

What blessing falls upon us as a royal priesthood![4] With God for us, nothing can stand against us – but relationships carry rewards *and* responsibilities. Our anointing came at a colossal cost at Calvary, as the true anointed one was crucified and stained with our guilt. David teaches us that following God, in denial of primitive needs, was a precursor for being lifted in God's eyes, aware of who we bring down. He shows us fundamental components for kingship, for ultimately his heart was tuned to God's and his people's victory, not just his own.

... you are a chosen people, a royal priesthood, a holy nation, God's special possession, *that you may declare the praises of him* who called you ... into his wonderful light.'[5]

1 Chr 10; 1 Sam 31; 2 Sam 1 [2] 1 Chr 16:22; 1 Sam 26:9 [3] Exod 17:16 [4] 1 Pet 2:9 [5] 1 Pet 2:9, italics added

BIBLE IN A YEAR: 2 Chronicles 24,25; Ephesians 5

A Time to Grieve

Lord God, show me your ways, but also show me where I have wandered from them. Where I have sought my will over yours, before you, today, I bow down.

The elimination of the army and the death of Saul were a tragedy for Israel.[1] This was a house divided, though it had formerly stood united before God, and it now faced the inevitable consequences. Israel's glory lies slain on the heights – in full view of its enemies. The mighty have fallen (v 27) – they were brave Israelites (the bow and sword did not neglect their duty, v 22), in spite of their shortcomings. Many in Israel may have questioned David's grief over Saul's demise, but David's elegy honours both the anointed Saul and Jonathan, whom he dearly loved. Later, David himself would find the temptations of kingship difficult to resist!

Today, we are called to be Jesus' ambassadors, inevitably facing times of difficulty and frustration yet commanded to love and pray for those who persecute us.[2] At times, we will feel alone or weakened, but God doesn't call us alone: rather, within a community, to walk in a Christlike way together. He calls and anoints us for his purposes, even when we don't understand. Initially, Saul the prophet had, like David, sought after God's heart. Sadly, his flesh consumed him, yet David and Jonathan had continued to pursue God's battle to restore unity. We all need to respect those who may not hold our opinions, yet still follow the Lord – this brings unity to his body.

The song in these verses calls for respectful honour: let the mountains mourn, let the earth and its people weep, for these men of God are dead. David's heartache is real (v 26), as must God's be. He chose Saul, he has chosen David, but ultimately, he can anoint whosoever he chooses, for it is not victory over lands or wealth he desires but peace and unity.

Saul and the Amalekite desired self-elevation. In David and Jonathan, we see a difference: love, one-mindedness and loyalty for each other and God. Who are we like?

[1] M Evans, *NIBC 1 & 2 Samuel*, Hendrickson, 2000, p142 [2] Matt 5:12,44

BIBLE IN A YEAR: **2 Chronicles 26–28; Psalm 74**

Where Shall I Go?

Jesus was killed like Saul, so he could reign like David.[1] Lord, teach me to follow your lead, to search after you wholeheartedly and with purity of heart.

After Saul's tragic fall and with his son (Ish-Bosheth) ruling Israel, God's people are divided. Many are loyal to the house of Judah, others are still loyal to Saul's line. But God is moving, as he always does with his people, just beyond our comprehension or time span. This passage opens 'In the course of time ...' How hard it is, when we desire God's plans and next steps, to face the frustration of preparation and the fullness of time. David's patience shows his heart and obedience. He asks God, 'Shall I go?' I am sure that, over the waiting period, he would often have prayed, 'Lord, what now?' Eventually the Lord says, 'Go.' Again, when many would have seen 'Go up' as enough, David once more seeks the direction of God: 'Where shall I go?' (v 1).

This is a challenge to us, as churches and individuals: do we seek God's direction when we hit the impasse, or do we ask it before we set out? David is sent to Hebron and he goes – obviously, we may say; but are there times when we know God is sending us to pray, speak or act for him but we close our hearts, allowing the flesh to quench the Spirit?

Hebron was important as the resting place of Abraham and his family and as the city given to Caleb as his inheritance.[2] This was a special place for the people of God, as they sought after God's heart, through trials and triumphs. This was home. David and his men were no longer fugitives. His loyal men, too, had suffered, but now they would reign with him. Holding unswervingly to God's way is often hard. Be encouraged – he is faithful.

What are your plans for today? Do they coincide with God's? Have you asked him, as 'Lord', for the day's directions, warnings and promises: 'Where shall I go, Lord?'

H Thomas and J Greear, *Exalting Jesus in 1 & 2 Samuel*, Holman, 2016, p176   [2] Josh 14:13

BIBLE IN A YEAR: **2 Chronicles 29,30; Ephesians 6**

2 Samuel 2:17 – 3:5

Brothers at Arms

'For the sake of your Son, Jesus Christ, who died for us, forgive us all that is past; lead us out from darkness to walk as children of light.'[1]

David's house rises while Saul's house collapses. With hindsight we can appreciate God's repositioning, but how God's heart must break as those he has loved, saved and covenanted with seem determined on self-destruction as brother fights brother. It's easy to criticise from afar. Often I have felt disquiet sitting in a service and thought that I can somehow do better, or that 'the church' needs my wisdom! It's so easy to bring division, to destroy rather than build.

Abner stood and questioned, 'Must the sword devour for ever?' (v 26). The enemy loves divisions within our fellowships and seeks to find any way to widen them.[2] We find it hard not to wield the sword of pride; it takes a godly heart to let the 'other' speak. As Joab says, 'If you had not spoken, the men would have continued pursuing them until morning' (v 27):

a difficult challenge to our path of righteousness and its outworking for God. So often the battles that rage are not with the 'enemy',[3] but within the body itself, as it reflects diversity in various states of glory into glory, each of us trying to live according to God while being very aware of the ever-present flesh!

Is it time to stop running? To stop to talk to one another and to God? To realise that the man who brought the young David to Saul after David had fought Goliath is the same man now fighting against David? The Philistines were the enemy. Somewhere along the way, God's people split and turned on themselves – and bloodshed followed. Stop running, stop fighting. Stand and face the ones you think are against you, for they are more than likely your brethren with the same heart, after the same God.

'If you keep on biting and devouring each other, watch out or you will be destroyed by each other.'[5] Am I still teachable, willing to listen?

---

[1] D Taylor, *In His Presence*, ASB/16, Wheaton & Co, 1983, p120 [2] 1 Pet 5:8 [3] Eph 6:12 [4] 1 Sam 17:57
[5] Gal 5:15, TNIV

BIBLE IN A YEAR: **2 Chronicles 31,32; Luke 1:1–38**

SACRED TRAVEL
PRACTICAL SHAMANISM FOR YOUR
VACATIONS AND VISION QUESTS

BY
KATIE WEATHERUP

A Hands over Heart Publishing book

Second Edition
First Printing
August 2019

Cover Design by Michele Jackson
Editing by Shannon Jackson Arnold, Kaliani Devinne, and William H. Stoddard
ISBN 978-0-9778154-5-6

TABLE OF CONTENTS

DEDICATION

To Mara Clear Spring Cook

Who not only is my best friend but also my cheerleader, travel companion, sacred mirror, wise woman, teacher, and space holder. I am blessed by your presence in my life.

INTRODUCTION

Approaching travel from the energetic as well as the physical creates a multilayered experience. For example, Death Valley is my earth altar. I am reborn and changed each time I go there. I watch tour buses drive through and feel amusement at the places that give tourists something to see and check off their lists. You see groups gather around the lowest spot in the northern hemisphere and the salt flats. I, on the other hand, am often pulled to stop at unmarked places along the road, where deep healing, wisdom, and gifts are offered. When I step out of the car, I experience veils that part and welcome me into the other side. There's a feeling of crossing a barrier into the more shamanic and essential nature of the land. For me, it's palpable. I can sit on the other side of these veils and watch tourists hiking along, following the routes that they are flowed along, getting only the smallest whispers of the energy that is coursing through my body.

It's just as well. The deep medicine of the places I travel can be too transformative for those who are merely enjoying a good hike with some great pictures. Shamanism can be called the Path of

Lightning. It's good to be aware that if you choose to dance with the energy of places you visit, deep healing, activation, and transformation often follow.

People travel for many reasons. As a shamanic practitioner, I have different reasons at the head of my list than the average tourist. I travel to connect to the energies of the land. I love the feeling of land vibrating beneath my feet, the sense of the power and energy of visiting sacred places. Those who merely experience the beauty of the places seem to be missing so much when they could be making their travel more powerful, magical, and meaningful.

This guide will help you connect more deeply to the land while traveling or at home. It will teach you how to meet the guardians of the land and invite their protection. It will help you deepen your energetic perception and discernment, allowing you to experience energy more profoundly when you travel. This book offers suggestions and practical advice for those new to the concept of "energy of the land," as well as ways for those with experience to expand their skills.

This guide will also support you in dealing with some of the challenge of traveling as an energetically sensitive person. When you're standing in a sacred power spot, being able to feel the energy run through you is a huge benefit. For me, it's the difference between a black and white movie and Technicolor. However, it can be less than fun if you're an energetically sensitive person standing on a piece of land that has seen bloodshed and pain, or in the mixed and psychically noisy experience of an airport. My goal is to support you in enjoying all the wonderful aspects of feeling a deep energetic connection to the land, while also mitigating the challenges.

In my experience, the soul, residing in the human body, retains profound connections to all that is—our soul history, our body, the world around us. I know many people don't resonate to the shamanic framework of understanding the unseen world. Yet, when people talk about places they have been and why they travel, I believe most people have the same core experience as I do. The person who doesn't believe in past lives or energy may still be in love with a certain place in France where I see them as having a past life or where the earth energy aligns well with their vibration. They will tell me how pretty the scenery is, how kind the people are, and how great the food. I will see their energy body being filled up with light and understand that it would be natural for people to be extra nice to them when they were filled with joy and happiness.

I believe that many who travel have sacred experiences when they find themselves on land that resonates deeply with their soul. I see people experience profound gifts of healing and insight as they travel, even if their conscious mind never takes in the information. When I visited the British Museum, my conscious experience was overwhelmed by so many powerful and diverse objects under one roof. I couldn't make sense of the experience. Yet I had several nights afterward where my dreams sorted through the activations and connections that happened by my being in proximity to these objects.

So why read this book if your soul will have the connection to the land regardless? I believe I can help you have way more fun and receive greater gifts on your travels. If you have a context for your conscious mind to make sense of what you're experiencing, you can have a fuller engagement of your being. You can engage your conscious intention with your soul in your quest for life experience. By working with the techniques I will teach, I open myself up to the following gifts:

- Coming into relationship with land—This connection remains long after I've left.

- Activation of gifts and abilities—The guides of the land often teach me new things and activate potentials I didn't know I had.

- Hedonistic experiences—Some of my most blissful moments have happened out on sacred land. You can get an orgasmic high in power spots.

- Deeper wisdom—I learn about myself and the world around me in my travels.

- Richness of life experience—When I was younger, I always thought traveling would be amazing. I love that I have gathered to me so many rich life experiences of seeing amazing places.

- Shamanic work—My Mesa, which is my portable shamanic altar, is assembled from stones from my travels. This supports me in my shamanic healing practice.

Series Vision

This ebook is intended as the first in a series. In this book, I talk about recommendations for travel that apply to many different places. My intent is to continue the series with ebooks specific to locations. I look forward to sharing stories about my travels in Hawaii and where to find ancient and mystical yew trees in Wales. The series will be for the armchair or shamanic traveler who wants to connect to faraway places without leaving home, as well as for the physical traveler who wants information on sacred places and energy hot spots in different locations around the world. If you sign up for my mailing list at www.handsoverheart.com, I'll identify one of your power animals if you wish (a great guide to connect with on your travels), and you'll get updates when additional books are released.

My Work

Travel is only a part of what I offer in my practice. Visit my website at www.handsoverheart.com for more on my offerings. I'm especially passionate about a process called soul retrieval. It brings back energy and power that you may have lost, disowned, or forgotten along your journey. A single session is often life-changing. It's wise to embark on travel from the most solid personal foundation you can create, and soul retrieval helps you gather your power and essence, giving you more personal resources for whatever you experience in life. I also offer custom journeys for people traveling places to connect them with the guides and track in the destiny path of a safe and powerful journey. For more information, see Appendix B.

I also think shamanic journeying is one of the coolest things ever. I love having a direct, personal connection to the divine and I'm passionate about teaching others. I also offer in-person and distance classes and training.

Travel with Me

Would you like to experience Sacred Travel with me? Imagine yourself hiking to the Sun Gate at Machu Picchu, greeting the dawn from the center of Stonehenge, or standing a foot away from the lava flow in Hawaii. I'd love to share this kind of experience with you. I offer shamanic retreats each year and am delighted by custom destination requests. I've set intent that this book helps bridge me to people who would like to travel with me. If you feel the call, please contact me at katie@handsoverheart.com.

When you travel with me, I can provide support for a lot of the things I talk about in this book. I connect with the guardians of the land before I travel and work with my guides and the guides of the land to weave protection and support around those I travel with. I put significant energetic protections in place for the daytime experiences, as well as providing space clearing and wards for the night.

And, most fun of all, I can offer shamanic ceremony, guided journey, and messages, in the moment, on the land. I track the energy of those I travel with, so if you do find that shadow stuff comes up or you need support, I can help balance your energy. I put a lot of attention on my retreats into weaving together the community spirit, so everyone is mutually supportive. If you're very drawn to the spiritual and energetic aspect of travel, it's a delight to spend time in community with others who are drawn to experience the same. I love the evolving, ever-moving magic that flows through this kind of deep experience.

If you sign up for my mailing list at www.handsoverheart.com, you'll receive information about retreats I'm leading. You can also contact me directly to explore designing your own trip. Sometimes I think one of my taglines should be, "Have Mesa, Will Travel."

CHAPTER 1: ENERGETIC CONNECTION WITH THE LAND AND GUIDES

Sensing the Energy

If you're reading a normal guidebook, it will tell you which flora and fauna are dangerous and how to protect your physical self and belongings. The idea is to support your having discernment about your physical environment in order to keep you safe and help you enjoy your trip. This guide is designed to support your having discernment about the energy of the places you visit. You probably already have good skills for feeling energy on a basic level that helps you discern whether you like or dislike a place. This chapter will help you to refine your perceptions a bit more and to learn how to increase your energetic sense of the land at will.

Many people I work with are more energetically sensitive and/or open than the average person. On the upside, this makes it easier for them to connect with the spirit and energy of the land, to access intuition, to receive messages, to feel things. I wonder sometimes about the person who drives up, takes a quick look, and goes on their way. So much of the richness of travel for me is about the energy of the land. Not feeling that seems like it would be akin to missing one of my senses.

Yet this energetic sensitivity can also create some complexity for me that other travelers don't need to worry about. If I don't take appropriate steps, I'm more likely to be awakened by ghosts, since I can perceive things more easily. It's wonderful to be able to open my senses and feel the pulse of the leyline through the land. It's less great to stand on the site of a massacre and suddenly feel all the pain, fear, and trauma.

If you're wondering if you're energetically sensitive, consider these questions:

Are you more intuitive, sensitive, empathic, or emotional than the average person? Do you sometimes have strong emotions that you can't explain? Are you sensitive to your environment, finding noisy, chaotic places uncomfortable? Do you know what other people are feeling?

Answering yes to some or all of these questions may mean you're sensitive to energy. If you get overwhelmed, shut down, or feel spacey when there's a lot of emotional intensity or high stimulus in your environment, you may be energetically sensitive. Without skills or training in managing energetic sensitivity, we often find way to try to shut it down, because in addition to whatever is going on in the physical situation, on some level, even if it isn't conscious, you're taking in a ton of information about the energy. Thus, many highly energetically sensitive people may not think of themselves that way.

Being able to have good discernment and good filters is an important part of connecting with the energy of places. Just because energy is powerful doesn't mean it's necessarily healing, friendly, or beneficial to people. I remember hiking out to a vortex in Sedona once and feeling rather awful afterward. When I tuned into the energy, I realized that the area in question was engaged in a powerful earth process of breaking down energy and transmuting it. This was a beneficial composting process for the earth. However, it wasn't the greatest place to put the highly organized human energy field. A less sensitive person might not notice the disruption of their energy field, but it was very unpleasant for me.

One of the first things I pay attention to is tuning into the question, "How does this place make me feel?" While it's true that sometime we can have an uncomfortable but beneficial experience, in general, I find the deepest healing happens on land where I feel welcome and invited. I look for feeling better in some way. Perhaps my emotions feel lighter, maybe there's a wonderful tingling feeling, sometimes I feel a delightful sense of being altered, like I've had a bit of wine. As you travel, pay attention to what land makes you feel good. A place can be powerful and sacred but not a match for you.

As I walk around outdoors, I often feel the sense of a tugging or pulling. Perhaps the left path feels more enticing. Maybe I'm drawn to stop and stand somewhere. My ability to sense and experience energy is very much increased when I'm standing or sitting still. I can feel some energy while I'm walking or driving, but stillness gives me the deepest experience. Sometimes it feels like a game of warmer/colder as I find the spot that's best for me to sit in. I also look for a comfy place, so if the overall energy is good and I want to sink in more deeply, I seek out a smooth rock or nice patch of grass. It may seem obvious, but it's easier to feel the energy of the place if you're physically comfortable—the right temperature, the right blood sugar level, and nothing sharp poking you when you sit down.

It's helpful to let go of getting it "right." One of the ways to push away this subtle sensing of what the land has to share and how we might move upon it is to get caught up in our heads. I remember doing a mini-journey quest several years ago. I was sitting on the cliffs above the ocean, inviting messages. My vision had gone internal, tuning out the world around me. I suddenly looked down at the ocean to find a huge pod of dolphins swimming in front of me, the light was luminous on the water, and the sky was full of birds. I felt the message so clearly that when I went inside my own head, I missed the beauty and gifts of the universe in front of me.

A good analogy is to treat your sense of the energy of the land like a shy child or animal you're trying to coax to come closer. You'd probably go still, speak softly, and say kind things. If you go self-critical, are too much in motion, or speak unkindly to yourself, this budding sense can slip away. The great thing about practice is that you can develop and strengthen this sense all the time, making it easier and easier to tap in. And you don't have to wait until a big trip to practice. It's good to spend time outside often and you can tune into your local park or the land you live on using the same methods as in an ancient stone circle.

In connecting with land, I often look for a space a bit off the beaten path. I find it easier to connect with the essential nature of land if it spends more time with the turning of the seasons and the movement of the stars overhead than with human beings. If I feel invited to do so, I'll often step off the main hiking trail or seek out a less traveled place to connect with.

Connecting with the Guardian and Making an Offering

A good place to start when you arrive somewhere is with an acknowledgment and offering to the guardian of the land. Whether you feel energy strongly or very little, you can still direct your intention in this way. I find that going through this process often results in an opening of energetic veils, allowing me to connect more deeply and perceive things that others may not be able to access. When I walk out onto the land, I often have a sense of stepping through some invisible curtain that has opened up for me. It's a sense of stepping between worlds to the more powerful, direct, authentic experience of the land.

In making an offering, I often let my intuition guide me. There are a number of traditional offerings, such as cornmeal, tobacco, and flowers. It can be valuable to research the customs of the indigenous people for what kind of offerings they make. The advantage to offering something traditional, such as tobacco or cornmeal in New Mexico or flowers in Hawaii, is that the guides easily recognize the intent. Rattling and drumming are used all over the world as a way to connect with shamanic reality and the guides, so when we beat a drum or shake a rattle, we connect with the bridging energy by participating in an action that is deeply instilled in the collective consciousness. The guides know it, our subconscious knows it, and the energy itself provides a gateway. So having an offering that's traditional in some culture and meaningful to you or that's traditional to the land you're visiting is a powerful way to connect.

In making your offering, find a place that feels right and place whatever you're offering on the land. As you do so, hold your intention in your mind. For example, you might think, "I make this offering to the guardian of this land. Thank you for this experience. I invite your blessing and protection. Help me hear your messages that I may walk with grace and honor upon your land." For me, my offering is often in the form of water from my water bottle. As a being whose physical body contains so much water, this is a good offering that relates to the organizing principle of life. Sometimes I make offerings that are a part of me. I might spit on the land, leave a strand of my hair, or, if I'm menstruating and have enough privacy, I might leave a bit of my blood.

Another way I make offerings is of my shamanic efforts. So I might offer to be the bridge for star seeds (energy from the cosmos that is being offered to the earth) by holding intent that they pass from the universe into the land. I can offer healing prayers and intentions for the land. For me personally, since helping souls cross over is a large part of my work, I will offer spirit release work, creating an energetic bridge for souls that have become stuck or lost. (Unless you're fully trained in psychopomp work, don't try to offer this. It's too easy for someone who isn't trained to end up with spirit attachments.)

After making an offering to the guardian of the land, I do my best to attune myself to what's in alignment for spending time there. Imagine you are visiting a friend's house for the first time. It would be normal to tune in to your host and hostess for cues about what would make you a good guest. Do they remove their shoes at the door? Do they seem to like things in order? With some people, you feel that you have permission to lounge on the floor and that it would be hard to offend them. When visiting others, you might be more mindful of the impact on their home. Some places are very welcoming of people doing whatever they wish. In other places, a more quiet, attentive, somber energy is a better way to engage. You might behave differently at the beach than in a church. The more you tune in and align with how to be on the land, the more secrets and gifts will be reveled and shared with you.

Invite yourself to sense the guardian of the land and see what comes to you about their nature. Give yourself permission to be wrong. Shamanism is about personal truth rather than objective truth. My experience of Pele, the volcano goddess in Hawaii, is different from what others have experienced of her. It is right and good that we connect with the flavor of an archetype that is perfect for us. You can delve in more deeply if you give yourself permission to tune into the guardian and play with whatever idea comes to you about the nature of this being. When we find a place that resonates for us, we often come into relationship with the guardian of the land.

Connecting with a Tree

One of the exercises I include in my six-month shamanic training class is communicating with a tree. Within the shamanic framework, we consider that everything has life and spirit. For this experience, walk among trees holding the question and intent in your mind, "Which tree has a message for me? Which tree wants to talk to me?" Walk and look around until you feel a tug or a pull. While you're doing this, give yourself permission to do it wrong. If this is a new way of opening your awareness, the intuition might be faint, which can have you questioning and second-guessing yourself. Nothing bad can happen (unless you fail to watch for gopher holes or the like), so give yourself the gift of space to explore and perhaps get it wrong. The ability to receive intuitive information is strengthened through practice.

When you feel a call to a tree, approach it and make an offering and thank the tree. For me, this generally looks like pouring a bit of water on its roots and saying "Thank you" in my mind. Then I sit with the tree. I might lean against it, sit among its roots, or sit across from it. I tune in and ask what the tree wants to share with me and what messages it has. Then I let things arise in my mind. This can feel like making things up, and that's okay. Just see what arises.

Sometimes I'll take a burden or pain to a tree. One of my shamanic teachers tells the story of having her back go out and being bent over with pain. Since her chiropractor wasn't open, she went to a tree and poured out all of her emotional pain and shame about her former drug addiction. She says she went from barely able to stand up, to walking away standing up straight and free of pain.

Trees are extremely balancing for the human energy body, with roots in the ground and branches in the sky. Ideally our energetic body resembles the configuration of a tree, with lines of energy (branches) reaching up above us to connect with source, spirit, and our higher self. Equally important, we send energetic roots down into the earth, connecting us with the planet. These roots feed us and keep us grounded and resourced on earth. I often work with clients whose energetic roots are very weak. This can lead to a lack of foundation, money issues, a poor sense of self, challenges with boundaries, and a lack of excitement about life. So hugging a tree can be used to reinform and remind your energy body of how to connect above and below in a balanced way. Because of the movement of energy through trees, they can help carry energy into the earth or up to spirit to be composted.

You can ask a tree for a healing. Generally I pick my intent—to ask a question, to receive a message, to release pain, to balance my energy body, or to receive healing—before I pick my tree. One tree might have a message for me, another might be chatty, a third might be all about offering healing when asked. So holding my intent in my mind when seeking my tree will affect which one I'm drawn to.

This process can be used with rocks, streams, mountains, and so on. In the shamanic framework, everything in the natural world has life and spirit and so this process can be used to connect with any part of the land you're on. It's a rich experience to access the great wisdom in the natural world that is available to us.

Vision Quest

A great practice when you travel is to allow time outdoors in a natural place for a mini-vision quest. I love living in this era in which we enjoy a higher vibration than what our ancestors experienced. To peek through the veils of separation and connect with spirit, our ancestors had to work a lot harder. Techniques such as fasting, sweat lodges, plant medicine such as peyote, or extensive meditation were needed to be able to hear spirit clearly. While these are things that still work and some people feel drawn to experience them, for those who prefer a path that is less taxing to the physical body and fits a bit better into a full schedule, we have the amazing gift of living in a vibration that makes connection to spirit very easy.

You don't have to fast for days alone on the land to connect deeply, get rich messages, and connect to spirit. When leading a retreat in Death Valley, Mara and I take people to power spots, give them instructions to connect in, and then in the evening, we adjourn to the hot springs retreat center where, after a good meal, we can share our messages in the hot pools before sleeping in a comfortable bed. We see profound changes in our own lives and in the lives of those who join us for this kind of extraordinary journey.

I recommend allowing at least an hour for a vision quest. Longer is better and you can do it in less time, but either way, you'll want to be able to really sink in. Start by making an offering to the guardian of the land. Then begin to just notice the attention of the natural world. Walk around and really see everything—the leaves, the grass, the spider webs, the ants. Allow your full attention to be drawn into noticing the natural world. As you walk and move, tune into how the natural world responds to you. As humans, one of our universal needs is for attention. Often the person or people we'd like to pay attention to us are not available for the way, timing, or quantity of attention we desire. So learning to have some of your need for attention met by spirit, as embodied in everything around you, is a way to have more balance and fulfillment in your life. It's breathtaking to slow down and notice the many layers, colors, textures, and life processes going on in the natural world.

Once you've shifted your way of perceiving the natural world, bring to mind your question. If you're not sure of a question, you can always use, "What does Spirit want me to know?" Begin to hold your question in your mind and notice what happens. The message may come in a bird crossing your path, which might say to you, "You're letting things get in the way of your ability to fly." You might see ants working and realize that persistence is needed. I like to do this kind of vision quest for deep questions, especially if I'm emotionally conflicted about them. When I have a profound internal conflict or lack of clarity about something, this is a powerful way to choose my path from my deepest truth. It's also a way to connect very deeply with the land I visit in my travels.

When you feel complete, thank the land, perhaps with another offering. As you go on your way, notice how you feel in your body and emotions. For better or for worse, as humans we experience the world through the mind and the thought stream. But as you walked on the land, asking questions and observing what came to you, you were also connecting at other levels. Often spending this kind of quality time in nature nourishes us and replenishes our being in ways that can be subtle or dramatic. I love the modern era, but I am keenly aware of the challenges we create for our body, mind, and spirit when we get too disconnected from the natural world. Just sitting in a resourcing place for an hour can realign our energy body, feed our soul, and support our physical body. When you do so in a place that has a profound energetic component and power, this effect is magnified.

One of my favorite things is to be in a powerful, sacred place that aligns with my energy and to have time to really sink in using the vision quest format.

CHAPTER 2: WORKING WITH THE HUMAN INFLUENCE ON THE ENERGY OF THE LAND AND PROTECTIONS FOR TRAVEL

One valuable thing to keep in mind when traveling is the complexity of human history. One of the sacred places that many feel called to visit is Egypt. Wandering through the British Museum and seeing the amazing artifacts, I could feel a powerful gateway into the energy. Many people connect with the mystical qualities of the Pyramids. Yet they often gloss over the fact that those pyramids were built with slave labor. So, however powerful the spiritual/mystical energies of places like the Pyramids, they were built by people who did not share modern sensibilities of "all men are created equal." Servants and loved ones might be entombed with the king. Builders were put to death to protect the secrets of the tombs.

It's tempting when looking at great works of art, temples of old, or things from the past to romanticize the indigenous people who came before. Many people feel out of sync living in cities, disconnected from the cycles of nature and the land. So it can be tempting to attribute great wisdom, grace, and evolution to indigenous cultures. Indeed, as a shamanic practitioner, I draw much wisdom and training from those who used this work as a primary form of healing.

In his book, "The Better Angels of Our Nature: Why Violence Has Declined", Steven Pinker presents a powerful case that we are living in the least violent times in human history. He looks at a number of aspects, from death by violence, to violence toward our children, and compares the experience of cultures throughout the world, past and present. For most of history, war, slavery, infanticide, child abuse, assassinations, gruesome punishments, deadly quarrels, and genocide were ordinary features of life. But today, Pinker shows all these forms of violence have dwindled and are widely condemned.

One of my favorite places in the world is Hawaii. The indigenous religion, before Captain Cook arrived, included a series of rules called Kapu. Violation of this ancient Hawaiian code of conduct of laws and regulations, even accidental violation, was often punishable by death. Rules included things like men and women not eating together and the shadow of a commoner not crossing that of a king. Living in a world with intense population pressure combined with active land including volcanoes, tsunamis, and earthquakes resulted in a superstition designed to appease angry, punitive gods. Nonetheless, the shamanic traditions of Huna still hold much wonderful wisdom and healing for the modern times. The result is that the shamanic wisdom of the Hawaiian Islands must be filtered to be aligned with the idea of a benevolent universe before it can be effectively used by the modern practitioner.

One of the aspects of shamanic culture that has been abandoned in its modern incarnation is the use of black magic. Modern practitioners of shamanism (as well as Wicca and other earth-based religions) have a strong sense of the ethics of honoring free choice and a commitment to "do no harm." Yet our shamanic and magical ancestors practiced curses, black magic, soul stealing, blood magic, and so on. Just as shamanic healing and earth magic was highly developed as providing the most powerful connection to the environment, black magic was used in warfare and competition for resources.

What does this have to do with traveling places? While it's a charming idea that indigenous cultures lived in grace and harmony with all that was until invaded or colonized by various world powers, the truth is more complicated. For the energetically sensitive, an awareness and understanding of this complexity can be very helpful in filtering the energies of the places you travel. It is wonderful to connect to the wisdom, power, and knowledge of those who came before. And it's wise to filter out that which we don't wish to invite forward, such as suffering, pain, injustice, and violence.

One of the things that I enjoy about connecting with power places and sacred spots from cultures that came before is that the connection to the land seemed to be much stronger. For example, the Neolithic people of Britain built stone circles at the intersections of powerful ley lines. Experiencing the sacred places of those who lived on the land long ago can bring us to places of immense power, earth magic, and healing. Bearing in mind the complexity of how humans interacted with each other can allow us to filter out the heavier, more painful vibrations and energies of the past, allowing us to connect only with the energies that are appropriate for us at this time.

So how do we create these filters? As in many kinds of shamanic or magical work, they are a matter of intention and focus. In creating my energetic protections and filters, I start by talking to my guides and the guardian of the land about what I want to experience. The request might run like this:

"I invite protection from my guides and the guardians of this land. May I have the experience that serves my highest and best good. As it is in divine alignment, please filter out any lower or painful energies from my experience. May the appropriate guides travel with me to keep me safe and allow me to have a rich, joyful experience. May I feel the energy that is right and good for me and receive whatever activation, blessings from the land, and healings that are in divine alignment."

It can be helpful to carry an object—a stone or a piece of jewelry—that is charged with the intent to provide protection. And, having set your intention and asked the guides for help, you'll want to periodically focus on this intention and remind yourself of it.

From there, be discerning. If everyone is very excited about a certain spot, and you approach it and start feeling nauseous, angry, upset, or unhappy, I recommend backing away and finding somewhere else to connect. It may be that the energy is just too intense for your system. It could be good energy, but being focused at fire hose pressure. That can be great for people who aren't energetically sensitive, since it allows them to feel something, but harsh and excessive for those sensitive to energy. Or there may be some level that you resonate to of the many layers of energy that isn't pleasant. Don't worry too much about understanding why, or whether anyone shares your truth. If you have a spot that makes you feel awful, find another spot. I find that if other people have the story that a given spot is "wonderful," it can make individuals ignore their inner truth that the place doesn't feel good. Our energy fields, soul histories, and such are so varied that one person's most magical spot may not resonate for me and vice versa.

Just as you can focus your senses on feeling more of the energy of a place, you can focus on feeling less. You can imagine yourself encased in white or golden light or a blue egg. You can call on your guides or the guardian of the land and ask that the energy be less intense. Imagine you have a dial that can be used to turn your energetic sensitivity up or down, making your energy system more open or closed. Practice playing with this dial so that when you're traveling and you run across energy that's not your favorite, you can turn down your connection to it.

Of course, far more often, I experience wandering into blissful places. I connect with the energy and feel amazing, happy, and like I could sit there all day. In well-known places, the spot I'm most drawn to isn't usually the spot that is known to be the center of something. For example, in Stonehenge, I was drawn to places outside the center. Sometimes the energy of a sacred spot will move a little bit over time. Sometimes it's harder to feel the energy if you're standing where so many people have had their own human experience of the place. For example, in Macchu Picchu, I felt far more connection sitting on the side in some of the agricultural terracing up above than I did by the sun temple. I think that was because I didn't have to connect into the energy through all the layers of meaning and experience that thousands of other people had. So give yourself permission to find a more psychically quiet spot off to the side. You may feel more energy.

In traveling we experience many different kinds of energy. So having good filters is a vital part of the experience. I want to feel the clear power of a ley line, but not the pain of battle and bloodshed even if both are connected to the same spot. The more you practice holding these kinds of filters with your intentions and focus, the stronger and easier they become to work with.

CHAPTER 3: TRAVEL PREPARATION

Past Lives

Often the places we feel called to travel to are places we've lived before. We can find ourselves someplace we've never been, yet have a sense of knowing the land. Perhaps we farmed land with dirt just that shade of red or stood on those cliffs, watching for a loved one to return from the sea. I often experience an evocative feeling in the places I visit that's out of context for what's happening in the moment.

Connecting to land you once lived on can be deeply nourishing and can add to your power and strength, especially if the lifetime there was happy and fulfilling. One of the great gifts of living in the modern era is the freedom to travel with speed and ease. We can change our location often. In other lifetimes, where you were born was a serious commitment. Although people did travel the world and there were many nomadic cultures, living and dying in the same place was common.

So coming back to a piece of land that nourished you in other lifetimes can feel like a deep homecoming. It can help you remember a part of your soul journey, often not consciously, but in some deep way. For example, if you were a great seer or healer or priestess on a certain piece of land, you can reclaim a part of that energy into this lifetime as is appropriate.

Or, by connecting with land that has carried a certain energy for many generations, you can activate the potential within you. For example, Glastonbury in the UK has a lot of connections to Goddess and priestess energy, making it a powerful place to awaken those aspects within yourself, whether or not you've had a past life as a priestess.

On the flip side, traveling to lands you've lived on before can awaken echoes of past lives that weren't so pleasant. It can take enjoyment out of a trip if your soul is remembering the lifetime you spent as a slave or when a loved one died of the plague. For most people, this isn't a conscious process, just something that can arise in unexplained or overly strong emotions.

When I'm taking a big trip somewhere, especially international travel, I'll often do shamanic work ahead of time in order to release and clear any past life pain that might be awakened by setting foot on the land. I do this in shamanic journey space. Feel free to contact me for a journey if you're preparing for a trip and want messages and past life clearing before you go. Another way to do this is with Fire Ceremony. See the chapter on Fire Ceremony for details on this process. Working with the guides to release and clear past life pain before you travel can help you have a wonderful time while you're there.

Shamanic Journeys for Travel

If you travel like I do, the moments of the trip are often full and finite in duration. So I have certain things I do to prep for a major trip before I arrive. In addition to putting movies on my iPad and researching the weather, I prepare energetically for my trip. For those who do shamanic journeying, it's great to do some shamanic journey work before the trip. You might do several journeys before your trip. If you'd like to learn how to do shamanic journey, my book, *Practical Shamanism, A Guide for Walking in Both Worlds*, provides detailed instruction.

It's good to journey to meet the guardian of the land before you arrive. By coming into relationship before you arrive, you can help anchor an easy flow of travel from the moment you get there. Being known to the guardian and under their protection is similar to having good friends somewhere you visit, who will pick you up at the airport, whisk you off to a great restaurant, and give you all the insider tips on what to see and where to go; as opposed to the folks standing at the curb, guidebook in hand, trying to hail a taxi and figure out how to get fed and to their hotel. Coming into Ayni or right relationship with the land and the guardian ahead of time can have chance and possibility working on your side from the moment you arrive.

When my friend Mara and I were traveling in Hawaii, we accidentally locked our keys in our room, which delayed us by about 15 minutes. It gave us the chance to talk to the concierge, who recommended a great BBQ place. We'd been talking about wanting BBQ the evening before, so that was wonderful. We arrived and Mara went off to the restroom. A man started talking to me in line and ended up buying us lunch and telling us about a great hidden beach. We went there after lunch and loved it. In addition to the gift of lunch and a great recommendation, I had been having a moment of feeling less pretty than my friend, so the fact that this man came up and was clearly drawn to me, in the nicest possible way, was an additional gift.

On another trip to the Big Island, a platform had been opened up to view the lava pouring into the sea. We'd gone a few nights before and it had been a walk of a few miles round trip because all the nearby parking was completely filled up. We decided to try going again, but agreed that we'd not do it if it was that long a hike in the dark. We hit traffic, which slowed us down, just to the point that we got a parking spot right in front. This was especially impressive because out of the 100 people there, only about 15 got the close parking. So having the guardian of the land conspiring on your behalf can magically help you meet the right people, find the right places, and have a magical experience.

Another great journey to do is to ask the guides what are the gifts and lessons for this trip and what to prepare for. I like to also ask if there's any healing or work I need to do before I get there that will make the trip flow better.

Alternatives to Shamanic Journeying

For those who don't resonate to shamanic journeying or who haven't learned yet, you can use the fire ceremony process to amplify your intention. You can ask for messages in the dreamtime. It's great to write these questions with your dominant hand (right hand for many people), and then write answers with your nondominant hand (the left for most). This will help you access your intuitive answers and you may be surprised at the results.

It's great to have those who love you send intent for your journey as well. The power of others intending you to have a good trip can help anchor that destiny path more strongly. I share about my travels on Facebook, partly because those who care about me help hold the vision of joy and success in my journeys.

All of this doesn't have to take a huge amount of time. But devoting an hour or two to this sort of work, perhaps spaced out into several intervals, can set you up for a more blessed travel experience.

CHAPTER 4: TRAVEL SHADOW WORK

One of the experiences I've had with sacred travel is that my unhealed stuff comes up. I find that I have more peace with it if I do everything I can to support myself in having the best possible experience, and then, once I get there, surrender to what is.

I love Elizabeth Gilbert's description in "Eat, Pray, Love" of feeling about travel as a doting mother would feel about her crying child. Even when it challenges her, or tires her out, or she's sick, she still adores it. As a highly energetically sensitive person, in some ways I'm not at all suited to travel. Airports are very psychically noisy, so it takes more effort to sustain my energetic shields and have a good experience. This means that I'm likely to be a bit more worn out than the average person after flying somewhere. Alas, I'm not one of those people blessed with above average stamina, personal energy, and vitality. I'm envious of people who can go with little sleep, miss meals, and still have energy and enthusiasm at the end of the day.

So, when I travel and experience all different kinds of energy, there's a profound richness to the experience, but it can also wear me out. Being Shamanic Girl, you'd think I'd adore camping because it's such a close connection to nature. The truth is, I can enjoy camping, but not sleeping in a normal bed, the lack of a shower and indoor plumbing, the meals I eat while camping — all these things are a drain on my energy. So, in order to enjoy camping and have fun, I need to go in with a lot of energy, and I will be paying back my energy bank afterward.

As a result, I usually make an effort to arrange my travel in a way that helps me conserve as much energy as possible. I try to have a bed to sleep in, indoor plumbing with a hot shower, healthy meals. But even with optimal self-care, being somewhere else can take you out of your comfort zone. I don't have the same freedom and choice if I'm traveling with others as I do at home, since there's a constant balance of the needs of the group with the needs of each individual. So it's easier to get my feelings hurt, feel tired, act grumpy, or get triggered. Travel is a great way to find places where you haven't really resolved an underlying issue; instead you've just arranged your life so that the buttons around that issue don't get pressed in normal circumstances.

When I travel, I often find myself getting to work with how I can manage my thinking and my energy in a way that creates the most ease—both with giving up control and in making wise choices for me based on what's available. Everyone has different needs and desires around having the most comfortable travel experience. However, in traveling, it's almost certain that at some point circumstances beyond our control will have things not going the way we would choose. Airplanes get delayed, meals turn out to be awful, we get the hotel room next to the noise and amorous couple with all-night stamina, the child next to us on the train decides to demonstrate their ability to wail for hours, or perhaps we get sick.

Whatever arises may be a challenge for us personally to roll with it, or perhaps the challenge is in staying in compassion with a traveling companion who is less zen about things. I remember a comedian commenting that anyone driving even a little bit slower on the freeway is an idiot and anyone driving faster is a maniac. Similarly, small differences in traveling companions that normally wouldn't be noticeable can turn into big triggers when we're tired, hungry, or sleep-deprived. As a result, I make sure I travel with people who are healthy enough so that being out of their comfort zone isn't likely to cause a major meltdown.

Beyond that, being able and willing to be uncomfortable and have emotions arise makes it easier when such things happen. I'd love to have my travel be purely about pleasure; however, my soul often chooses deep healing and transformation. I am changed by the places I go, and growth and change, especially when they happen quickly, are seldom comfortable. I find a lot of mirrors when I travel, in the people around me and in being able to see things about myself. Something unhealed may be at a low volume when I'm in my comfort zone, but I might vividly see where my inner control freak or judgmental side emerges when things are outside it.

When uncomfortable emotions arise, anger, sadness, fear, frustration, I find that it's most helpful to go into them, rather than trying to push them away. In going into them, I can start with a key question, "Is this mine?" In asking that, I make sure that I'm not resonating to what's unhealed on the land or in another person I'm traveling with. Even if I carry the flavor of the wound somewhere, if the majority of the emotion is an activation from energy outside myself, it's wise and kind to activate my filters so I don't end up trying to process the land's or someone else's healing through my personal emotional matrix.

One of the ways you can make yourself truly crazy in travel is unwillingness to surrender to what is before you, rather than what you want to be experiencing. If we've spent money and vacation time and put a lot into going on a trip, and we get a major button pressed, the pain of wishing we were having fun while we're actually dealing with uncomfortable emotions or shadow work can be excruciating. So setting intent to deeply meet whatever arises in your travels is very helpful. If you go in knowing things might be stirred up and willing to meet whatever experience is there, it is much easier to move through an emotional storm and back into sunny weather.

I have a number of techniques for dealing with strong emotions. I've included a modified excerpt from my book, *Sex, Shamanism, and Healing: My Kissing Quest* in Appendix A to provide more information and support for dealing with shadow emotions.

CHAPTER 5: AT NIGHT

One of the challenges of traveling for the energetically sensitive is the nighttime. As we drift off to sleep, our brain drops into altered states of consciousness. In fact, in shamanic journeying, we use a drumbeat of 3–5 beats per second to induce theta waves in the brain, allowing us to drop into an altered state of consciousness. When we fall asleep, we go through the theta state.

This means that all the filters we have to let us perceive only the physical reality of our world can come down, allowing us to perceive the energetic truth of the world around us. This can result in an experience of weird, disruptive dreams and discomfort. Before I learned to put up protections in my hotel room, I often had strange, disrupted sleep when I traveled.

When sleeping somewhere unfamiliar, anyone who tends to have disrupted sleep or strange dreams while traveling might do well to do some basic space clearing and put up protections for the night. I recommend these practices at home as well; however, the approach when traveling is a bit different. It needs to be quick and efficient—

after all, at the end of a long day, you don't want to engage in an elaborate ritual just to go to sleep. And when traveling, you need to be able to do it without having to take along a bunch of props.

If you're camping somewhere in nature that spends more time open to the elements than inhabited by people, you don't need to do space clearing, just move on to protection. However, if you're sleeping where lots of people have lived or slept, you'll want to start by cleaning out the old energy. I recommend starting by simply turning your attention to the place where you're sleeping and imagining what the energy is like. It may feel fairly clear or you may feel uncomfortable with the energy. This gives you an idea of how much focus to put on this step.

The simplest, fastest of doing space clearing, which requires no props, works on intention and focus. Sit quietly, take a few deep breaths, and center yourself. Then speak your intent to your guides, the divine, or whatever spiritual allies resonate for you. For me, this might sound like, "I call upon my guides, Star Beings, Power Animals, and Angels, all those who serve my highest and best good. I ask that this space be cleared of all energies that don't serve me. Please clear anything that doesn't serve and bring in good energy to support me in having deep and restful sleep." The effectiveness depends on your ability to affect energetic change through your intention.

It can be helpful to combine this with shamanic tools. I often travel with a stick of Palo Santo, a sacred wood from South America. It is very powerful for personal smudging (which helps keep my energy clear) as well as space clearing. It also doesn't give off a lot of smoke, so there's much less chance of setting off the smoke alarms with Palo Santo than with sage. Open a window before smudging a room; it lets the smoke out and gives the energy you're clearing an easy path to leave. Light the Palo Santo and move around the room with it, holding the intent to clear the energy. Smudging to clear energy rather than using your intent alone is more effective because the nature of how Palo Santo interacts with its environment leaves the space energetically clearer. Even someone who isn't holding any intention in their mind, but who just waves around a burning stick of Palo Santo, will leave a space clearer than before.

You can use a small bowl of salt to absorb any negative energy or a candle to provide ongoing protection. One of the most important aspects of space clearing is finding something that resonates for you. There are many, many methods of clearing energy; a simple Google search will reveal many options. Choose something that feels good to you, that can be done quickly and easily, with portable tools. It's great to practice at home, both since it's always good to keep your space clear and so that you'll feel comfortable and confident when doing it in your hotel room.

The next step is creating protections for the night (or nights if you're staying in one place multiple nights). When I travel I always try to book the same place for multiple nights if possible. I like being able to sink in and not have to drag my luggage around every day. Also, you only have to do your space clearing and set protections once, unless you have problems sleeping in the night.

My framework for understanding the unseen world says that there are beings that aren't in bodies. My spirit guides and the guardians of the land are part of this. There are also the smaller spirits of the land, such as fairies and ghosts of those who have died and not gone to the light. There are also energies that aren't beings, but have a substance. For example, even if all the souls are released from a battlefield, there might be a lingering flavor of the energy.

The more work I do on my healing/shamanic path, the brighter the light of my soul becomes. So, when I travel somewhere, beings in that area can get curious about me. I don't want a lost ghost waking me in the night asking for help to find its way, or the fairies of the lake coming to see what kind of being I am. Admittedly, there are those who are less of control freaks than I am, but I'm protective of my rest, a much nicer person when I sleep well. I'm also very determined that I will interact with the unseen world on my own terms. So, when I put up my protections around my bedroom, or the house I'm staying in, or my tent, there are two intentions. One is simply to provide a barrier so that anything that's not on the side of my highest and best can't come in. The other is to put up a layer of concealment, so that I don't show up on the energetic as a big, bright, interesting light while I'm trying to get a good night's sleep.

One of the goals with wards or protections is to get them in place so I don't have to think about them anymore or use my energy to sustain them. I find it helpful to travel with objects that will anchor my shields. I have a quartz crystal that I fold wards into and pop up (like a pop-up tent) when I arrive at my destination. I leave the crystal out. When I leave, I fold the wards back into the crystal and wrap it up. However, creating such a thing is an advanced technique.

You can create a small crystal grid or have a stone or crystal that provides protection that you take out. I've created a mini-travel mesa, with very small stones, that provide protection and power when I travel. One way to put this together is to look for stones, either outdoors or in a crystal shop, and ask which ones will provide protection and want to be your warding stones. See where your eye is drawn. When you pick up the stone, see if you feel more protected and safe. You can also look up stones that are good for protection. Lay these stones out in a grid (or just however feels right) while asking your guides for protection. You can also visualize or imagine a sphere of light that surrounds the space you're in, with a cloak over it. Having a mental picture of the protections around you helps anchor them.

This may seem like a strange process, in which you're using your imagination to clear energy and create protections. For a number of people who aren't energetically sensitive, this process may seem strange and unnecessary. I invite you to experiment with it. If you get better sleep while traveling by setting energetic protections and doing space clearing, great! If you find it doesn't make a difference, then it may not be needed.

Just as I far prefer to stay in a hotel room that's clean and attractive, I feel much better if I sleep in a space that is energetically clean, clear, and infused with light, in a place that's protected. For women especially, having energetic protections in place can help our instincts be more relaxed. However much I may enjoy being out and about, there's a part of me that relaxes inside my home, with its protections in place. Allowing my instinctual self to get good rest at the end of a day tromping about in sacred travel makes the next day far more enjoyable.

This being said, even with perfect protections and wards, you may still have deep, intense dreams while you travel. The dreamtime can be a space where energy, teachings, and transformation from being connected to the land unfold. You can let the guides know your preference about this kind of work in the dreamtime, but when I travel, even if I've asked for deep sleep, sometimes I get intense work in the dreamtime because that's when I'm most open to the land. Putting in good protections and doing the space clearing helps ensure that this work is taking place with the supervision of my guides, for my highest and best good, and not merely the result of getting bogged down in someone else's story who slept there previously.

CHAPTER 6: TOOLS FOR TRAVELING AND FIRE CEREMONY

Shamanic Travel Kit

When I travel, there are some things that support the spiritual and energetic aspects very well without taking up too much space or adding too much weight to my suitcase.

My traveling shamanic kit includes the following:

- iPod
- Travel Mesa
- Small stick of sage
- Palo Santo
- Fire ceremony kit
- Objects for wards
- Things to offer to the land
- Tea lights
- Compass

The iPod: In addition to all the great music, it has my shamanic drumming recording. This allows me to take a journey any time I can create a bit of quiet space for myself, without my needing to take a drum or a rattle. I also put a rainstorm track on there so I can plug it in and create white noise at night, which helps me sleep.

Travel Mesa: My normal, full size Mesa is larger than my hiking boots and weighs more, so it's not great to put in a suitcase for international travel. So I created a travel Mesa with stones and other objects that is about the size of my fist. When I'm at home, my travel Mesa lives with my full-size Mesa, so the two form a connection. This allows me to be directly supported by the travel Mesa and to connect to the full Mesa at home from a distance.

A small stick of sage: While it makes a lot of smoke, so it needs to be used in indoor spaces with care, if I need some major energetic clearing, it's great to have along.

Palo Santo: I travel with a stick of Palo Santo for my main smudging tool. You light the end on fire and move it through the space you want to clear, or your own energy field. Often when we travel, we pack a lot of experience into a short space of time. Alternately, a peaceful vacation can give you space to release energy that no longer serves. Either way, being able to clear your energy field quickly and easily is going to give you the best experience of the day and night. Alternately, you can bring some salt for a salt bath or scrub for personal energetic clearing.

Fire ceremony kit: My fire ceremony kit contains a metal tin with a three-inch diameter, filled with about a half-inch of Epsom salts. I also bring a small, spillproof bottle of 91% isopropyl alcohol and a book of matches. Note: This can't go in your carry-on luggage on a plane; in your checked luggage is fine. I use the match both as my "twig" to blow my intentions into and as the means to light the alcohol on fire. Then I drop the match in and let it burn. The kit doesn't take up much room and it gives me the power to create a direct energetic intervention around whatever is needed, be it my mood or my intent for the day.

Objects for wards: Small crystals or objects that help anchor a protected space. This could be Feng Shui fu dogs or a crystal grid. I use these to create a protected space for the night.

Things to offer to the land: I usually carry some tobacco, cornmeal, and small crystals as my default land offerings. If you have the inclination, it's great to research and see what offerings are traditional in the area you're visiting. There's a resonance to all who came before you and came into relationship with the land if you pick a traditional offering. So the connection happens more quickly and more strongly. That being said, it's about intention. So I might offer food to the land, knowing it will nourish creatures that live there, flowers to acknowledge the beauty, a strand of my hair to give something of myself, or water from my water bottle, since life thrives on water. Whatever you carry, it's also wise and good to make offerings before collecting stones or objects from the land to take away with you.

Tea lights: It's great to be able to light a candle for many reasons, and tea lights are highly portable. Since Palo Santo can take a little while to light, having a candle flame to ignite the stick can be very helpful.

Compass: If you are working with sacred space, it's great to know which direction is which when you call them in. In my experience, you can still call in strong sacred space without a compass, but being able to understand which direction is north can help you drop in more deeply with the land and feel oriented, no matter where you are on the planet.

About Fire Ceremony

The fire ceremony creates a direct energetic intervention. It's a simple process and a tool that is valuable for someone new to shamanic work as well as the advanced practitioner. When talking to the guides, adding in fire ceremony is like going from standing with your cell phone in an area with limited reception, to popping up your own cell tower on the spot. It amplifies your intent tremendously.

In sacred travel, fire ceremony can be used for

- Setting intent for the trip before leaving
- Working on clearing any traumatic or painful past life energy before you go
- Setting intent during the trip
- Clearing energy, within yourself or the space you're staying in
- Dealing with any challenging emotions that arise while traveling

The following write-up is for a fire ceremony specific to travel. It's also a highly effective daily practice. For more information on using fire ceremony to change patterns and life circumstances, visit my website at www.handsoverheart.com and go to "Fire

Ceremony" on the "Articles" page. If you prefer an audio format, I talk about fire ceremony in the May 2012 Practical Shamanism podcast show on The Shamanic Voice: www.theshamanicvoice.com.

You will need the following supplies:

- Epsom salts
- 91% alcohol (lower percentages won't burn properly)
- A fire-safe container such as a pie tin or ceramic dish
- A trivet or other heat-resistant pad to fit between your container and the surface you set it upon
- Matches or a lighter
- A stick or twig—select one small enough to fit in your container. A piece of sage, a matchstick, or a small paper with your writing or drawings on it can be good alternatives to the stick. The item must be safe to burn.

The element of fire provides a fast, visible means of releasing and healing strong feelings and experiences. We can also use fire as the catalyst for turning over our prayers and dreams of manifestation to Spirit for fulfillment.

The fire ceremony allows you to transform strong emotion through the fire, instead of through your own emotional matrix, providing accelerated relief from painful emotions. It is a way of disrupting habitual self-criticism and inviting in accelerated change. The fire provides a direct energetic intervention that allows you to reprogram your energetic field and soul blueprint.

Fire ceremony also is a form of self-hypnosis. The ritual speaks directly to the subconscious, allowing the change to be taken into deep levels of your being.

How to Perform a Fire Ceremony

Open Sacred Space: You may call in the Four Directions and Earth and Sky if that is your preference, or pray, or whatever works for you to create a sense of safety and connection with higher energies. This part sets the tone for the effectiveness of the ceremony. See the section on Sacred Space for more information.

Be Protected: Have a friend or one of your guides be "at your back" for you for this ceremony. You are revealing your deepest nature to shed your old skins and invite change, and at that moment you are vulnerable. Request this protective presence to cover your back for you. You can call in a Power Animal or Star Being for this part.

Set Intent for Your Ceremony: What do you wish to release today? What issues are you working with? Call up the feelings, the monkey-brain thoughts, worries, fears—whatever is occupying your energy. What do you want to invite in?

Create Your Fire Pit: Pour about half an inch of Epsom salt into the fireproof container and set it on a heat-resistant trivet or pad that will protect the surface below it. You can reuse this salt over and over; just crumble it should it form a crust.

Blow into the Stick: By blowing on the stick we are sending energy away from our own energy fields and into the stick. Tell the Universe what you are releasing and then blow into the stick. For example:

"I release my fears about travel."
"I release any painful past lives from the places I will visit."
"I release my anger, sadness or pain."

Blow and speak until you feel complete.

Also blow into the stick your desires and vision. Ask to fill the spaces within yourself that you are clearing with loving, higher vibration:

"May I hear the guides clearly, receive healing, and be protected physically and energetically in my travels."
"I invite meeting helpful people and seeing wonderful places."
"I invite the guides to filter out any energies that don't serve me, so I can connect with the aspect of the land that serves my best experience."
"I enjoy safe and pleasant journeys."

Make sure your requests are aligned with good energetic ethics, such as honoring the highest and best and the free will of all concerned. For example, it's okay to ask for a romantic relationship with a wonderful partner, but not to ask for a certain person to come into a romantic relationship with you. It's okay to ask to release the painful energy you are holding onto and for you to come into harmony with others. It's not appropriate to request that others' attitudes, actions, or feelings change by using the tool of fire ceremony.

When you are ready, pour a few tablespoons of 91% alcohol over the salt. Then light it with a match or lighter. You can use a wooden match as your stick, and then use it to ignite the fire. Never add more alcohol to a burning fire—the flame follows the vapor trail right to your hand and can hurt you or start a fire outside the container.

Drop the stick into the fire. Then brush your hands over the fire and toward you, as if you were scooping sand or water from a bowl. Bring the energy of the burned stick toward your belly. Draw again from the top of the flames and into your heart, then your throat, your third eye, and then into your crown. Always practice fire safety; watch for sleeves, hair, and other items. Don't get too close to the flames.

While you draw the changing energies into you, focus on thankfulness. Being in a state of gratitude facilitates quick and easy change as well as a right relationship with the Divine.

Stay with the fire until it goes out. It could take five minutes, or it could take longer. We are letting the fire do its business and there is no rushing it. Do not blow out or smother the fire. Let it burn out naturally. If you must step away, leave the fire container in the sink or shower so it can keep burning safely.

When the process is complete, close the sacred space by thanking the Four Directions, Earth and Sky.

More on Sacred Space

One of the greatest tools we have for connecting to spirit and to land is the ability to call in sacred space. The concept of sacred space is one that seems to be universal. For some it is a place of worship, like a cathedral. Others find places in nature to be sacred. Often a place in nature is held as sacred across many generations. A well, a grove of trees, or a stone circle marking ley lines becomes a place to do ritual and receive gifts from the divine. People go to these places to connect to spirit.

When I travel, I am drawn to places that have been identified as sacred. Given the choice between visiting a castle or a stone circle, I'll opt for the stone circle because there's a good chance the energy that resonates in the circle will make me feel better than the castle. Castles are cool and amazing to see, but I can't say they have great energy on average. Life was pretty cramped and uncomfortable in castle life within the feudal societies that built them.

Places in which people focus, again and again, on the divine and spiritual aspects of life take on an energy from that focus and connection. In San Diego, I have a healing space where I work. After years of my teaching classes, doing healing sessions, and working there, most people feel the energy of the space the moment they cross the threshold. Some feel it vividly; others just report that it feels "nice" or "relaxing." This is in a room in a building with no special energetic aspects.

So imagine a similar use of a space that already has energy and magic of its own. If you start with a place where two ley lines come together or water bubbles up from the earth, or very old trees grow, and then add on not just a handful of years, but centuries of people coming there with sacred intention, the energy is powerful and palpable. If you're new to sensing energy, attempting it in these kinds of places can be your best gateway to connecting to the energy.

I believe that healing, inspiration, personal growth, wisdom, and activation are all available to us in the natural world. Even a mundane but attractive park can offer these things. When we go outdoors, our energy bodies can realign with the energy of the earth. When people spend most of their time indoors, their energy field can get out of sync with the natural environment.

For human beings, being incarnate is an experience of separation from each other. Having our essence anchored in space and time opens up many gifts of unique experiences we can create. But it also is the origin of the primal wound of being human, which has us feeling lonely, alone, isolated. When the rhythm of our days moves us too far from the rhythms of the natural world, we can exacerbate this wound of feeling alone and isolated. We become too strongly influenced by the human collective consciousness, where we share and amplify this experience of separation, and we lose our unconscious connection to the natural world and the heartbeat of the earth. In fact, in my shamanic work, the first step in calming anxiety and turning off the fight or flight is to reconnect my client's heart to the heartbeat of the earth.

In addition to the sacred spaces we find indoors or outdoors, the shamanic tradition allows you to create sacred space anywhere you go. A simple Google search will give you many ideas of how to call in sacred space, or you can choose your own process. My approach involves addressing each of the four directions—South, West, North, and

East—in that order, as well as the earth below and the sky above. When I call to the directions, I call to Serpent in the South, Jaguar in the West, Hummingbird and the Ancestors in the North, and Eagle and Condor in the east. This style comes from my Munay-Ki training. However, there are many ways to call in the guides.

Moving into Sacred Space tells the guides we are open to their messages and want to connect more deeply. It allows us to create a protected energetic container anywhere and at any time to meditate, journey, or just be inside.

If you open Sacred Space, make sure you remember to close it when you're done. Not closing Sacred Space can leave you feeling spacey and in between worlds.

CHAPTER 7: WHAT YOU BRING HOME

One of the core reasons I travel is to come into relationship with land in different places. This relationship to the land lasts long after I've climbed in the car or boarded the airplane. When I leave, I take away the gifts and medicine that have been awakened inside of me.

In Hawaii, I connected with the energy of lava and received the energetic gift of lava in my belly from Pele, the volcano goddess. This energy of molten earth amplified my personal life flame, giving me more passion and creativity and helping to burn away what was old and stagnant in my sacral chakra. In the UK, I connected with sacred yew trees and received the energy of timelessness. Ireland's largest stone circle transmitted teachings about leadership and my role as a practitioner. Peru connected me to the Apu, the sacred mountains, and allowed me to come into deeper harmony with the divine masculine.

I come back changed each time I engage in travel from this perspective. I learn about myself and my place in the world. I receive new energetic gifts. I release energies from past lives that no longer serve and awaken power and connection that I developed in other lifetimes. The time I spend out on the land, in all these different places, teaches and transforms me. Just as I take pictures, there are all these energetic snapshots of places I've been.

It's valuable to create some space and time to journal about the messages and experiences of your trip. Often when someone asks me, "How was Death Valley?" or "How was your UK trip?" I stumble over the answer, because there are so many layers of experience to speak to that I can be left without words. I will often pick a moment and describe the place, the feel, the energy, and the messages rather than trying to encompass the whole. For many of us, the world moves really fast and after we've shared with our loved ones and moved back into the flow of life, the memory of the gifts and messages becomes dimmer.

One of my trips to Hawaii brought me onto Mauna Kea on the Big Island. I was struggling with the energy I was receiving from an ex who was very angry at my departure from our painful relationship. I made an offering to the volcano and the unbelievably huge masculine guardian came into a paternal role with me and offered to receive whatever energy was being sent to me that didn't serve. I felt profoundly held and protected. Writing about the experience at the time helped to anchor the memory. I have so many land guardians I can call upon for support, it's easy to forget when years have passed since the experience.

In addition to photos and writing, you may want to bring home objects from the land from your travels. A stone from a place you have been is steeped in the energy of that land and can provide a stronger energetic pathway if you want to reconnect to the feeling of being there.

In the shamanic and many other earth-based traditions, we recognize everything as having life and spirit, including the rocks, the dirt, water, plants. And we learn to interact with these essences, to come into right alignment and harmony with them. So, when you choose an object to bring back home with you, it's important to have permission to take it, both from the guardian of the land and from the object itself. Sometimes a stone or object is very happy being part of the energy where it resides. It's happy to have you notice it, pick it up, connect, but would prefer to be put back down. Sometimes it has a purpose for being in a certain place.

Before I gleefully pocket an object from the land, I tune into the question of whether it's okay to take it and whether it wants to come home with me. Often I'll get a yes, but sometimes a no. With practice, you get better and better at feeling into these kinds of answers. If I get a yes or a feeling that it's okay, I will make an offering to the land. This might be water from my water bottle, or something more formal such as tobacco or cornmeal. It completes an energy cycle by making an offering. Don't worry if you occasionally forget these steps; most often if we have good intentions the land is gracious if we forget to make an offering in our excitement.

Shamanic Mesas

Over time, as you gather stones and objects from places you travel, you may feel called to bring them together in a Shamanic Mesa. A Mesa is a shaman's power bundle, their portable altar. There are many different ways to approach putting together a Mesa. I invite you to play with what feels right. If you want to weave in a more traditional approach, that's wonderful. But just because some people have a number of rules for how a Mesa should go, I hope that won't deter you from creating whatever resonates for you.

I have three different Mesas. My travel Mesa is a small bundle that fits easily in a suitcase. My main Mesa is about the size of a basketball when it's bundled up. I also have a larger Mesa in the rocks and boulders that have come to me in my home and yard.

While each level of Mesa contains stones that have been purchased, many of the stones I have come from lands I have visited. They create an energetic link, so if I need to help someone release lifetimes of despair, I can send it to Death Valley to transmute. If I want to hold a higher vibration, I can use the rock from Mt. Shasta to connect with the vibration I want to anchor. By gathering together these stones from places I visit, with the permission of the stone and the land guardian, I create far more resources for myself in my shamanic practice. Rather than using my own energy, I can use my intention and my relationships, both to the helping spirits and to sacred land, to accomplish my work.

You don't have to be an expert or a practitioner or having any training to begin your own Mesa. It doesn't have to be used to support other people. It can merely be a collection of objects that connect you to or remind you of energy that supports and empowers you. At some of my most painful moments, I've curled up with my mesa on my lap and just let it work while I cried. It made the duration of those times so much shorter.

CHAPTER 8: LAND HEALING

It's always good to leave the campsite cleaner than you found it. This is great when we're talking about an actual, physical campsite, as well as a metaphor for our participation with the rest of the world. When I travel, I like to leave the energy of the land in better condition than I found it. Sometimes this calls for land healing.

There are many places in nature that don't need land healing. The land is full of life force energy, in possession of a strong guardian, and in alignment with the connections to those who live on it or visit. However, there are pieces of land that are not thriving as fully as they might. For a much deeper exploration of the concept of Land Healing, I recommend Sandra Ingerman's "Medicine for the Earth." This topic deserves a whole book, and she's written a great one.

Just in going through the process of making an offering to the land guardian and tuning into the places you visit, you can be healing for the land. If the spirit of the land has been dishonored in some way, your honoring can be healing. You can work with visualizing health and balance for the land you visit. Consider holding the vision of love and healing for the water in particular. Water responds very quickly to vibration.

Fire ceremony can be done on behalf of land for healing. Use the stick or twig to blow in your healing prayers for the land.

When doing healing work for the earth (or anything for that matter), do it with love and compassion. If you dwell on how the earth has been misused or damaged, you may find that you take on that energy or begin to feel depressed or heavy. For the time you're being of service, it's important to put aside the anger or resentment that you may feel about how people have engaged with the earth. Bring your best intentions, your love and your light, and offer them in service to the natural world. The energy will be magnified and reflected back.

More advanced shamanic work can be done by those trained to work with shamanic journeying. As I mentioned, I often do spirit release work and talk to the guardian about any work that the land would like done. If the land has lost its guardian, I may call in a new one. Soul loss can also happen for land, so sometimes I work with a version of soul retrieval. If you want to attempt more advanced work, make sure you have training and a good relationship with your guides. This kind of training is something I offer in my practice. It's important to have a strong team of guides and clear communication with them before attempting more advanced work because if you don't have the right protections in place, the energy can overwhelm you.

CHAPTER 9: HOW TO TRAVEL WITHOUT LEAVING HOME

While I love the experience of having my feet on the land, getting my physical self to my chosen destination can be a complicated endeavor, with expenses in time, energy, and money. Using shamanic techniques to travel to the destination of your choice can be much more affordable and timely.

My book, *Practical Shamanism, A Guide for Walking in Both Worlds*, provides detailed instructions for shamanic journeying. I offer distance and in-person training. For details, check out www.handsoverheart.com. Another great resource for this training is the Foundation for Shamanic Studies (www.shamanism.org).

For those who don't have a background in shamanic journeying, I'll offer a few suggestions about safely connecting with faraway places you want to visit, from the comfort of your home, as well as a few safety tips. For those who are familiar with shamanic journeying, I have more specific suggestions about how to apply this work.

Traveling to Spain or Bali in the format of a shamanic journey is a Middle World journey. This means that you're traveling in the energetic aspect of the human and earth realm. Middle World, the energetic aspect of the world around us, is the most complicated of the three worlds (Middle, Lower, and Upper). There are many beautiful experiences to have in Middle World, but it's also a place that includes ghosts and other entities. Just as when you travel somewhere physically, you want to connect with the wonderful, delicious, healing energy of the place, but not the pain, suffering, and earthbound souls that may reside there.

The best way to do this is not to try to send your awareness and energy to a place (unless you have proper shamanic training), but use your intention to invite the energy to come to you. It's best to make this journey indoors to avoid distraction. You'll be able to relax more deeply if you don't have to monitor your environment. Pick a time when you won't be interrupted, and turn off the phone.

Begin by calling in sacred space. This sets up protections for you so you can relax and enjoy the feeling of connecting. The guides can then filter out anything that doesn't serve.

It's helpful to have something to focus your attention on the place you want to connect with. This could be a travel guide, pictures of the place, or even the name of it written on a piece of paper. If you'd been there you may have travel photos or be able to picture the place clearly enough that you don't need this kind of anchor.

The next step is optional, but can increase the connection. Consider making an offering to the guardian of the land for the place you want to connect with. This could take the form of a prayer for healing for the land or a statement of gratitude to the guardian. You can place a traditional offering in a bowl. This could be cornmeal, tobacco, a flower, some water, a stone. When you're done, you can leave the offering out in nature somewhere.

So, here you are, inside of the sacred space you've invoked. You have something to help you focus on the land and have made an offering if you so choose. At this point, find a comfortable position to sit or lie down and close your eyes. Begin breathing deeply and slowly, relaxing. You want to get into a peaceful space. If you're experiencing anxiety or stress, you'll want to either pick a different time to do this work when you're more peaceful or do whatever calming practices allow you to feel centered, such as meditation.

Once you are feeling relaxed and centered, begin to focus on the place you want to connect to. You can visualize or touch the picture. Keep breathing and ask the energy from that place that serves your highest and best good to come to you. Be very clear that you're inviting the energy of the place to come to you so you can feel it rather than "going there."

Pay attention to what you feel. You may begin to see images or have information come to you. Perhaps you'll feel energy moving through a part of your body. You might get warmer or colder. Allow yourself to have the experience. Periodically come back to your intention to invite the appropriate energy from the place to come to you so that you can connect.

If you are struggling with this, check your breathing. Come back to breathing deeply and slowly into the belly and relaxing the tension in your body. Then return to the process.

For some, this kind of practice comes very easily. For others, the results may be subtle. In either case, the more you practice, the more vivid and in-depth your experience can become. For a place that you've been to before, this process is even easier, since you can see it in your mind's eye, while inviting your physical and energetic body to experience again what it was like to be there.

When you feel complete, thank the place you were connecting to and the guides. Then close sacred space.

I recommend not doing this while you're under the influence of a mind-altering substance. While shamanic drugs can be a powerful way to connect, in order for them to be safe, you need someone experienced and skilled to hold the container and/or in-depth training. It's tempting because you can experience things more strongly by taking down certain barriers. There are a couple of risks with this. The first one is soul loss. If you travel to some amazing place energetically, part of you may not decide to come back.

While in theory it sounds great if part of you could always be sitting on a white sand beach, the reality is that people with major soul loss have an extremely hard time being effective in their lives. It scatters your personal magic and power, so it feels as if the world is acting upon you, rather than you being able to dream your world into being. Also, if you leave a part behind somewhere else, you lose touch with it, so the enjoyment of the white sand beach is lost to the rest of you that still has to go to work, just with less energy and fewer resources.

The other risk of opening pathways to other places while on drugs is that you can pick up entities or soul fragments from other people. While these aren't the end of the world, they can linger and cloud your energy, while depleting it. A healthy, normal human energy field has great protections from this sort of thing. A person who is stoned or on drugs takes down barriers that provide these protections, creating vulnerability. A qualified shamanic practitioner can clear entities and retrieve soul parts, but we tend to advocate prevention.

For those who have read my book or studied shamanic journeying and feel comfortable with the process, you can use this to send your awareness to the places you want to experience. As I mentioned previously, this is a Middle World journey, so it's a slightly more advanced journey than the ones to Upper and Lower World. You'll use your shamanic drumming recording (with call back) for this journey.

To prepare to travel to places in shamanic reality, begin by calling in the guides who will travel with you and keep you safe. Do a journey to your sacred garden with the intent to meet the guides who will support you in this. They may be power animals or they may come in human form. Spend some time getting to know them. Make sure you trust them and feel safe with them. If you don't, you can ask for different guides to work with you. Henceforth when you travel to a place you want to visit, you'll always travel with your guides. It's their job to protect you from any energies that don't serve you. This being the case, if you ever ask to travel somewhere and get a "no" from your guides, it's important to honor that.

Once you've set up your team, you're ready to begin visiting places. With this new skill, moderation is important. It can be tempting, since you're riding the drumbeat, rather than an airplane, to the destination of your choice, to run all over in a single sitting. If you connect deeply with a place, allow yourself a day or more to integrate the experience. This isn't a hard and fast rule, but it can be uncomfortable if you have the energy of many powerful places move through you too close together, and it can diminish your ability to receive and anchor the gifts offered to you.

Start your journey by traveling to your sacred garden and meeting your shamanic travel guides. Then set your intent for the place you'd like to go and ask them to take you there. You may see a path you can walk down, or a thread you can follow. Or you may simply find yourself in the place you wanted to be. Until you arrive, keep holding your intent for where you want to go, and for wanting to go there with your spirit guides. If there's a path to follow, travel down it.

Once you arrive, experience the place. You can meet the guardian and offer thanks; you can play in the water or on the rocks or lie on the land. Invite the perfect energy to move through you. This can be a challenging journey because it's a journey that includes a lot of "being" in the experience, rather than a directed experience as when asking for an answer to a question.

When you feel complete, or when the drum call back sounds, travel back to your sacred garden, thank your guides, and then come back into the here and now. With this journey, pay extra attention to the process of coming back, making sure to gather all your energy and essence as you return. It's important to honor the drum call back when it sounds and come back, even if you reset your drumming and travel right back. The reason is that you want to make sure your muscle for coming back is at least as strong as, or stronger than, your ability to travel out. If you ignore the drum call back, you give the parts of you that might not want to come back the message that return is optional, and getting all the way back is harder.

I work with many energetically and psychically gifted people who are living their lives partly out of their bodies in spirit. The reasons vary, from not feeling safe in the world to current life circumstances they don't enjoy to pain in the body. The catch-22 with this is that the more you're not in your body, the harder it is to have health and vitality. Being out of your body will make you chronically tired, and that makes it hard to make the changes or have healing happen that would make your life more pleasing.

Connecting to land from a distance can be an amazing way to resource yourself. If you've traveled and found places that are "yours," that your energy, heart, and mind resonate strongly to, being able to pull in that flavor of energy and the resources from that place is a huge gift. I use my connections to places such as Death Valley and the Chalice Well to invite in energy when I get tired or emotionally drained. It's a good place to release stuck energy. Having journeyed there many times, in the physical and energetic, I have a relationship to the guardians, so I can turn on my drumming, travel there quickly, and be embraced by the energy in minutes. Each time I go there, the relationship deepens. We may not be able to run away to open spaces whenever we want, but finding a 15–30 minute window is often much easier.

It's also an amazing way to get energetic downloads and experiences with land that we haven't had the chance to visit physically. Often when someone talks about a place or I read a guidebook, I get the flavor of the energy. Stepping in more deeply, I can receive gifts of connection to land even when I can't go there. I invite you to think of these forms of energetic travel not as better or worse than physical travel, but as their own, stand-alone experience.

CHAPTER 10: THE LAND WHERE YOU LIVE AND MOVING

When you're considering a move to a new home, whether it's across the country or just to a new apartment, it's good to consider the energetic alignment of the new place. It's certainly possible to clear dense energy from the previous occupants, appease an angry land guardian, or help a few ghosts to move on. But it's an easier path if you pick a new home that has energy that's well aligned with yours on land with a supportive guardian.

In one of my advanced classes, everyone was having such a great time that we extended the class by three months and held a session in each participant's home. This gave us the chance to do land healing journeys and meet the land guardians in places all over San Diego County. It was interesting to find which places were very much in alignment with people living there and which were not.

If you are an energetically sensitive person, how you are aligned with the energy of your home and the land you are living on can have a huge impact on your quality of life. I worked with a couple some years ago who were having issues with their home. I did spirit release work with the souls of the Native Americans who had been killed there and worked with the land guardian to make peace with the people living there. My clients were instructed by the guides to make regular offerings to the land guardian to come into right alignment.

A few years later, the same couple contacted me. They were looking to buy a house and wanted a shamanic check before they finalized the offer. I was able to look at how the property worked with their energy, make suggestions to balance it better, and give them a full report on what was wonderful and what would need some work. It made me think that back when more cultures held with shamanic traditions, people didn't build homes without checking in with the shaman about whether the place was in alignment with supporting humans in that way.

If you're looking at moving, or especially buying a home or property, I invite you to contact me for a journey regarding the alignment. I can fix many issues, such as doing spirit release work as needed, as well as talk to the guardian on your behalf. I can also tell you how well supported you'd be living in this place. Occasionally there's a place that has so many layers of misaligned energy that it's going to take tremendous effort to keep the energy clean and clear. This doesn't happen often, but if this is the situation, it's often easier to move than to try to shift the energy.

You can also work with this yourself. It's good to take an offering to the land and find a place at or near your prospective new home to tune in to. Ideally, find a place where you can sit undisturbed, make your offering to the land guardian, and tune in. When you sit on this land, what do you feel in your body? Do you feel a sense of well-being or tension? Does it feel like a place where you can feel grounded or do you feel spacey? Sit with the question of "Is this a good place for me to live?" and see what happens. You may get signs in the clouds, in the animals that come by, in thoughts that rise to the surface of your mind.

If you want to connect more deeply with the land you live on, you can also use the mini-vision quest format. Pick a question to ask such as, "How can I be in the best alignment with the land I live on?" "Is there anything the guardian of the land would like to tell me?" "What are the messages from the guides about my land?" It's best to pick one question. Make an offering to the land. Then walk or find a place to sit, holding light attention on the question you've selected. As you walk or sit, notice. Notice how your body and emotions feel, notice what plants and animals you see. If you see a sign, an animal crossing your path or a leaf pulling your attention, ask yourself, "What does this sign mean to me in regard to my question?"

Consider that the land you live on knows you well. The plants and trees and fairies witness your way of being in the world. So connecting with the land you live on can reveal rich information.

Messages come in interesting ways. I was visiting Harbin Hot Springs one fall, sitting in the warm pool, when I watched a beautiful leaf fall from the sky into the water. It had stunning color. I picked it up, admired it, and when I moved to set it down, I felt that it wanted to stay with me longer. So I placed it in my hair. As I sat in the pool, I watched a man giving a watsu session to a woman. It was beautiful to witness. When I exited the pool our paths crossed and he spoke of how lovely the leaf was in my hair, which allowed me to tell him how beautiful it was to witness his session. He immediately offered to give me a session of my own. The session was profoundly healing and the first time I noticed feeling so full and gifted that I didn't have a single longing for something else.

Conclusion

Thank you so much for taking the time to read my book. I hope you've found value. If you'd like to know more about me and my work, please visit my website at www.handsoverheart.com. May your journeys be blessed and supported. May you find deep connection and much joy in the places you wander.

APPENDIX A: WAYS TO DEAL WITH STRONG EMOTION

The following is an abbreviated expert from my book *Sex, Shamanism and Healing, My Kissing Quest*, on how to deal with strong emotion.

I've worked with a lot of techniques for dealing with uncomfortable emotions. It wasn't a natural skill of mine, but I quickly found it vital to having the kind of life I want. Feel free to pick and choose whatever works for you.

"Anger: Wisdom for Cooling the Flames" by Thich Nhat Hanh offers a great way of dealing with strong, difficult emotions. He talks about taking care of the anger (or other feeling) as though it was a baby. By being present with the emotion, holding it, honoring it, being concerned with it, the feeling is resolved and released. His instruction is clear and loving. He provides wonderful instructions for meeting yourself.

I'm also a huge fan of Pema Chodron's Tonglen instruction. She has a number of books and CDs. The Tonglen practice is particularly wonderful for people who struggle with strong emotions. As we become aware of the difficult energies created by dwelling in pain, metaphysical seekers can get panicky when they find themselves stuck in anger or sadness. If we understand we manifest with our emotions, it can be scary to have these feelings that might undermine our goals for abundance and joy in the world.

In the Tonglen practice, instead of trying to get rid of uncomfortable feelings or push them away, you go directly into them. So, for example, if I'm angry at my boyfriend, instead of avoiding the feelings by telling stories about how he's bad, or having a drink to avoid the feelings, or trying to push them away, I breathe into the anger. Perhaps sadness or fear come up and I breathe into those as well. With tonglen, on the in breath you breathe into the painful feeling and allow yourself to feel it fully. On the out breath, you send relief to yourself and everyone else who is experiencing the same emotion. It's a beautiful practice that reminds us that we are not alone in our most painful moments. It allows us to shift our energy between the pain and the higher intent, which helps the energy of the emotion to flow and change and release. It is a great relief for me to find a way to be with my anger, judgment, and woundedness in a way that is spiritual and connected to the universe. I seek relief for everyone by embracing my own pain.

Tenderness toward the Self

Just being present with the feeling and thinking about it in terms of where you feel it in your body, what it might look like, how it might change over time can be a good way to help release strong emotions. All too often, when we're upset, we tend to make up stories, remember past events, and say things to ourselves that cause more pain. Even if it's true that your current relationship mirrors something from your childhood, when you're hurting, it can be better just to sit with the purple and black lump than tell yourself how you're always abandoned.

Inner child work is extremely powerful for dealing with strong emotions. Imagine that you're the parent you wish you'd had. Get an image of you holding yourself in the way that you'd like to be held. Allow that part of you to have whatever feelings are there and say the kind of loving, tender things you'd say to a child in pain. Like, "Honey, it's okay. I love you. I'm right here. I'm going to take care of you. I know it hurts now, but this will pass. I'm not going to leave you. You're safe." You may be amazed at how some tenderness toward yourself will help relieve these feelings. If you're struggling to find a grown-up part of yourself, you can call in guides or power animals or the divine to hold you in your pain.

I find it helpful to make a list of people that I trust with my vulnerable self at a time when I'm feeling good. When I'm hurting, it's easy to feel utterly alone. When I travel, it's good to have people I can call or write if I get bogged down in emotions during my trip.

In their books and recordings, Esther and Jerry Hicks talk about the Emotional Scale. The idea is that no one can reliably go straight from misery to joy. You need to raise your emotional vibration a little at a time. So if you hurt, instead of trying to be happy the next moment, you might think about ease and relief. Anger is an emotional step up from depression, for example. It may be more uncomfortable, but it's more life-affirming.

I get a lot out of Byron Katie's work. Her method is one of asking four questions that are very powerful for dismantling the painful stories we tell ourselves. It helps me to not take things personally. For example, I might feel, "My boyfriend doesn't love me." I would ask myself it that's true and whether I can absolutely know it's true. I then acknowledge that I don't know if it's true. I examine who I would be without that thought. I then turn it around and see if other things are equally or more true. "My boyfriend does love me." "I love me." "I don't love me." It's a method that breaks down painful stories and belief systems and helps me to make peace with reality.

Sometimes dealing with a strong emotion can be as simple as breathing into it and following the breath. Richard Bock has a great CD called Quantum Light Breath that is a wonderful guided journey of breathing and releasing. Without a sound track, or someone to hold space for me and help me stay on task, I find it very easy to lose track of my intent for breathing into the feeling. When I lose focus I can wander off into stories and mental distraction, so I like having the CD.

Being in Your Body

Coming back to your body is very helpful. One of the things that happen when we get used to running a certain emotional program is that we fall into the groove of telling ourselves a painful story, reacting in a certain way, and getting stuck. This might happen to someone who gets cut off on the freeway or thwarted in some way, who always responds with the thought, "You can't trust anyone. People will always hurt you." This thought and reaction get worn into a groove, so finding ways to disrupt those kinds of ideas and victim thoughts can create a powerful healing and life change.

Physical movement and exercise are great for transmuting strong emotions. When you move the body, you move your energy and it makes it hard for painful emotions to get stuck. It's difficult to be deeply depressed with regular exercise. Meditation or shamanic journeying can also be great ways to move your energy and state of being, allowing the peaceful release of challenging emotions.

One of my students shared her technique when she gets angry of visualizing a monster in a room that throws a fit and destroys everything around it. It creates a safe space to allow the feeling to be expressed, without taking it out on those around her.

Whatever technique you find works for you, I strongly recommend doing it with a conscious intent to transmute and release the energy back to life force energy. By spending some of your intent on cleaning up the energy you release, you won't find yourself bogged down in it later. This could be burning sage, playing music, lighting a candle, taking a salt bath, or using some other technique that makes you think of releasing and clearing old, unhelpful energy. Also, it's very important to make sure that you're not sending your painful energy to anyone else. My book, *Practical Shamanism: A Guide for Walking in Both Worlds*, deals with this in greater detail.

For a directly shamanic approach, I often use fire ceremony. Another technique I offer training in, called a "Decoupling," is used to turn off the fight-or-flight response.

Taking Action

For me, the challenge with any of these techniques for dealing with my strong emotions is getting myself to take action. To release and clear these emotions, I need to become present with them and acknowledge them, which is the opposite of my instinct to run away from pain. It takes a lot of discipline to be present with myself when I hurt, physically or emotionally. So, whatever baby steps you're able to take in this regard, remember to pat yourself on the back and honor your courage. And don't hesitate to take a class or find another person to help facilitate this process. The rewards are huge: more energy, greater joy, ease in setting and holding boundaries, increased self-esteem, and more grace in the world.

It's wise to be practiced in these techniques before you travel, so that you have established approaches to work with when strong feelings arise.

APPENDIX B: SOUL RETRIEVAL

Soul retrieval offers effective and lasting healing in one session for the following:

—Fatigue
—Depression
—Lack of passion for life
—Grief and trauma
—Feeling as if you don't belong
—Unresolved issues

Shamanic healing and soul retrieval also support

—Feeling secure in who you are
—Living in your power
—Speaking your truth
—Finding your passion and soul purpose
—Gentle and accelerated healing

Shamanic healing and soul retrieval can assist in attaining life goals, restoring health, and releasing old behavioral patterns and emotional and psychic pain. It can help to relieve symptoms of anxiety, depression, fatigue, and stress.

Many of my clients find shamanic work immensely helpful in gaining clarity about issues such as career, relationships, and their soul purpose or life lesson. Shamanic healing can be used to address the spiritual aspect of illness—whether physical, emotional, or mental. It can increase the effectiveness of other forms of healing, including regular medical and psychological treatment.

Shamanic healing works with your essence energy, which can be described as your soul or your spiritual self. It encompasses the intangible aspects of your being, including gifts, qualities, and aspects of who you are.

In creating a healing opportunity, it is useful to do healing work on the soul or essence level first. The soul or essence is the blueprint that tells the other levels of your being (your life force energy, your mind, your emotions, and your body) how to be. It informs the universe around you what type of relationships and experiences to manifest. Shamanic healing and soul retrieval are very effective tools for working on this level.

Because this work takes place outside space and time, it is possible to perform shamanic work from a distance. I record all sessions.

Shamanic Healing and Soul Retrieval

Life's traumas, dramatic or subtle, can cause portions of one's vital life force to become separated, creating dramatic imbalances in our lives. Symptoms such as depression, fatigue, memory gaps, or general dis-ease can receive profound healing through soul retrieval. When performing soul retrieval, I journey into the shamanic world, retrieve these separated soul parts, and return them to my client. Soul retrieval is one of my favorite healing techniques and one of the most powerful. One session is generally enough to address all past experiences of soul loss and can leave the recipient with unprecedented levels of vitality and wholeness.

Soul loss is part of the human experience. It's designed to protect our essence from physical and emotional trauma. Psychologists refer to this as dissociation. The shamanic community calls it soul loss. Either way, it helps us to survive.

Trauma that causes soul loss can be subtle and different for each person. Being teased or shamed can cause a sensitive child to lose soul parts. Another type of soul loss occurs when a part leaves because it doesn't fit or because it is sent away.

Soul loss can happen when parts of our soul are taken by or given to the significant people in our lives. People who have had soul parts taken unknowingly take soul parts from others. While there's no judgment or blame, this does put people in an inappropriate energetic relationship.

In a romantic relationship, people often will trade soul parts. This exchange makes both people more dependent on each other, less able to stand on their own, and thus less likely to leave. It can feel safer and more connected for both parties, but both are diminished.

Whatever the source of soul loss, the effects are much the same. Soul loss will diminish a person's sense of well-being, vitality, and joy in life. People often feel depressed, listless, and as though the world were all gray. Soul loss can lead to gaps in memory. People can feel fragmented or spacey or even as if pieces are missing. Sometimes people become accident-prone or keep falling into the path of misfortune. People with soul loss can spend a lot of energy working through events of their past and still feel impacted by them. In extreme cases, soul loss can cause a lack of sense of self, suicidal tendencies, and vulnerability to physical illness.

The emotional impact of soul retrieval is very gentle. Even when parts are lost due to severe trauma, they come back unharmed. After your soul retrieval, you may find it much harder to accept situations where you are not being honored, regardless of the economic or emotional advantages of being in that place. If you get soul parts back from another person, this can impact the relationship. In some cases, returning the soul parts instantly improves the relationship. However, any relationship where the other person is invested in controlling my client is likely to be made rockier by a soul retrieval, because it makes the recipient stronger and harder to control or manipulate. For people who have left a major relationship and are finding that they are having trouble moving on, a soul retrieval can help a great deal.

In a shamanic healing and soul retrieval session, I start with a power animal discovery to identify and connect my client with two power animals. Power animals are spirit guides in animal form that provide a connection to primal life forces, protecting and guiding us in the physical and spiritual world. Discovering and forming a relationship with your power animal may alleviate conditions such as lack of energy, tendency toward mishaps, or feelings of vulnerability. Likewise, a relationship with your power animal can provide support and guidance through major life transitions.

I also connect my clients with their personal Star Being, their personal "energy angel" that protects them, empowers their abilities to shield themselves from unwanted influences, and helps amplify psychic and other abilities. Your Star Being assists you in understanding and working with your own energy and energetic connections. This enhances your sense of your human self as a very important individual aspect of your entire soul, always connected to the whole, yet precious as an incarnation here on Earth.

Next, I look at the overview of my client's soul or essence and consult with the guides about anything that is out of alignment besides soul loss. Often the guides have me heal contracts or past life wounds or realign the energy field. If there has been childhood or past trauma, I often go back to those events and work to release the energy in shamanic reality to remove the energetic anchor of that painful experience. I also do extraction work as needed, removing spiritual and energetic intrusions. Then I do the soul retrieval work, bringing back the pieces that my client has lost. Finally, I consult with my guides for information about whatever specific issues my client has mentioned — relationships, career, money, soul purpose, etc.

Sessions vary, since whatever work I do is directed by the guides. My sessions are designed to provide a profound healing that is completed in one session.

Because the work is occurring on the soul level, how this experience translates to the conscious human level varies from person to person. It's not unusual for these sessions to be described as life-changing. Sometimes the results are very subtle, increasing strength and wholeness. The session takes about an hour to an hour and a half. Current information may be found on my website at www.handsoverheart.com.

BIBLIOGRAPHY/RECOMMENDED READING

Practical Shamanism: A Guide for Walking in Both Worlds, Katie Weatherup. San Diego: Hands over Heart, 2006.

This was my first book. There are worlds of healing, protection, and insight available to you just beyond ordinary reality. The knowledge to simply, powerfully journey to these worlds, to connect with your spirit guides, to build a vision of yourself as healthy, intuitive and psychically alive, is within this book. Whether you are just beginning to seek a truer and more meaningful existence, or you are an experienced traveler of worlds, this book provides a reliable, straightforward, friendly, and practical guide to basic shamanic practices, including more advanced instruction in past life healing, shadow work, and soul retrieval.

Sex, Shamanism, and Healing: My Kissing Quest, **Katie Weatherup. San Diego:** Hands over Heart, 2009.

You are invited. This book is a kiss and tell. It tells stories of fun, juicy sexual experiences, long, sweet kisses, whispered words and touches in the dark, all offering the reader delicious vicarious experiences. It is also a roadmap to healing for survivors of sexual trauma. It offers new pathways, hope, and wisdom to make that journey swifter, more pleasurable, and more complete than following only the more conventional routes to healing. This book is a guide to women's empowerment, to finding, embracing, and actualizing the feminine divine within. It's a journey to finding and joyfully claiming your power, complete with detailed exercises and instructions. This book speaks to healing between men and women. It offers ways to mend the gap between the sexes and open to a balance in which both are empowered, honored, and whole. This book is an invitation. Come and play.

The Dark Side of Light Chasers, **Debbie Ford. New York:** Riverhead Books, 1998.

This is the best book I've come across dealing with shadow work.

Loving What Is: Four Questions That Can Change Your Life, Byron Katie and Stephen Mitchell. USA. Three Rivers Press, 2003.

I have found Byron Katie's books tremendously helpful in unwinding my painful thinking.

Ask & It Is Given, Jerry Hicks and Esther Hicks. USA. Hay House 2005.

Esther and Jerry Hicks channel Abraham, providing simple, loving, straightforward instruction on the principles of energy, manifestation, and creating the life you desire. It's a 101 kind of guide to the spiritual world.

When Things Fall Apart: Heart Advice for Difficult Times, Pema Chodron. USA: Shambhala, 2005.

Pema Chodron's books and CDs, such as this one, provide loving, beautiful instruction on Tonglen. Tonglen is one of the most powerful practices for transmuting painful emotions that I have experienced.

Medicine for the Earth: How to Transform Personal and Environmental Toxins, Sandra Ingerman. USA: Three Rivers Press, 2001.

This book covers the basics of shamanic journeying. Sandra Ingerman has also written Soul Retrieval and Welcome Home, which are excellent books related to soul loss and soul retrieval.

The Journey to the Sacred Garden: *A Guide to Traveling in the Spiritual Realms*, Hank Wesselman. USA: Hay House, 2003.

This book also covers the basics of shamanic journeying. In addition, Hank Wesselman deals with how to explore and use your place of power to affect change in your life.

Shaman, Healer, Sage: *How to Heal Yourself and Others with the Energy Medicine of the Americas*, Alberto Villoldo. New York: Harmony Books, 2000.

This book has good information about right alignment and right relationship to the universe.

Psychic Protection, **Ted Andrews. USA:** Dragonhawk Publishing, 1998.

Ted Andrews is one of my favorite authors. His writing is clear, accessible, and filled with compassion. I recommend this book for anyone who is feeling nervous about the unseen world or who is looking for ways to better manage the energy they take in from the world around them.

CLASSES AND WORKSHOPS

I offer a number of workshops and seminars. For the most up-to-date listings, visit my website at www.handsoverheart.com

Learn Shamanic Journey—In this one-day class, I teach students to do shamanic journeying to meet and connect with their guides.

Meet Your Star Being—In this 1–2 hour class, experience a guided journey to meet your Star Being, an energetic guide to help you manage energy and awaken your gifts. Meet your Star Being is also available as an .mp3 download.

Spiral Wisdom—This six-month journey involves in-depth shamanic training, Reiki training, and personal healing.

A Shamanic Experience—I lead shamanic retreats in various locations, such as Hawaii, the UK, Death Valley, and Peru.

In addition to my training, I recommend the following:

Mara Clear Spring—A gifted teacher and practitioner in her own right, students and clients often work with both Mara and me. www.maraclearspring.com.

Foundation for Shamanic Studies, www.shamanism.org—The foundation offers excellent shamanic training in locations throughout the world.

Acknowledgments

I am deeply grateful for many ways that I have been supported on my own personal healing journey as well as the journey to this book, by beings both in physical and in nonphysical form. As regards the physical ones, thank you first to John Honeycutt for suggesting that this book take its current form and for conveying such excitement and vision. It inspired me to move forward on the project. Thank you to Mara Clear Spring Cook for giving me the timely nag I needed to focus in on completing the project when I got distracted. Also, for being my co-facilitator on so many of my retreats.

I deeply appreciate all the people who help my writing flow better and who have provided their help with proofreading and editing. In particular, Shannon Jackson Arnold, Kaliani Devinne, William H. Stoddard, Helen M. Westerlund-Davis, and Marie Scott. I appreciate your gifts of time and skill. All errors and non-standard usages are my own contribution.

Thank you to all those brave souls who have let me lead you somewhere on retreat. As of the writing of this book, I've had the joy and honor of leading groups to Death Valley, Peru, Hawaii, Ireland, England, and Wales. These times hold some of my most treasured memories.

ABOUT THE AUTHOR

Katie Weatherup is a shamanic practitioner, a Reiki master, and a former mechanical engineer. Her unique perspective on shamanism centers on the application of each person's spiritual and intuitive abilities to the issues attending everyday life from a pragmatic, "what works" point of view. She helps people find their way back to themselves, all the parts they have lost, forgotten, denied, and disowned. Katie helps people realize new levels of happiness and fulfillment in a single session and to form a direct, personal connection with the divine.

Shamanism is a staple of her healing business, Hands over Heart. Currently residing in San Diego, Katie offers distance healing sessions and soul retrieval to clients all over the world. She also teaches classes in shamanism via her online academy. Katie's "Practical Shamanism Podcast" is available on the major podcast platforms. For more information, visit her website at https://handsoverheart.com.

Printed in Great Britain
by Amazon

44225329R00067